THE END OF ANXIETY

"If you are reading this because you are looking for help in dealing with fear, anxiety, and panic, I know you aren't looking for shallow answers or advice from someone who doesn't know the depth of what you're going through. You've already had enough of that. Here's a book that will point you to a clear path out of the darkness, and every step has the solid foundation of Scripture underneath it. You'll have no doubt that the author identifies with your pain and struggle and that the counsel he offers was forged from many long experiences in the Refiner's fire."

> —**Donald S. Whitney,** professor of biblical spirituality and associate dean at the Southern Baptist Theological Seminary in Louisville, Kentucky, and author of *Spiritual Disciplines for the Christian Life* and *Praying the Bible*

"The apostle Paul said that 'in the last days difficult times will come' and then described the culture of that period (2 Timothy 3:1–5). Whether you think we are in the last days or not, you have to agree the times in which we live have prompted a pandemic of anxiety, fear, and worry. Pastor Josh humbly admits his own struggles in these areas and clearly points the reader to the life-giving, hope-inspiring truths of Scripture. He writes with the warmth of a struggler who has found answers for his own soul and is eager to pass on what he has learned. Biblical counselors will appreciate not only the clear biblical exposition but also the practical suggestions for implementing the truth in one's life."

> —**Randy Patten,** director of training emeritus for the Association of Certified Biblical Counselors (ACBC) and president of TEAM Focus Ministries

"Fear is the darkroom where negatives develop. The destructive force of fear is felt in every aspect of our lives. Fear paralyzes potential. Fear replaces hope with anxiety. Fear limits our lives, all while making us emotionally miserable. No wonder the phrase 'fear not' is in the Bible 365 times—one for every day! The question is, how do I drive fear out of my life? With grace, humor, and devastating transparency, biblical counselor Josh Weidmann will take you with him on his own journey through anxiety and offers along the way not only the solid truths of the Word that became milestones for him, but practical actions you can apply to your own life. Read this, apply it, and find freedom from fear—forever."

—**Ray Johnston,** senior pastor of Bayside Church in Granite Bay, California, author, and president of Thrive Communications

"We live in a world that gives us more and more reasons to be fearful and anxious, but Josh Weidmann takes you by the hand and walks you through his own personal battle, sharing the good, the bad, and the ugly as God's Spirit has taught him how to 'fight the good fight of faith' (1 Timothy 6:2). His biblical and grace-filled strategy was not worked out in the comforts of his study but in the deep, dark trenches of his own personal battle with fear and anxiety. The pages are filled with the humble, transparent wisdom of one fellow sufferer telling another where he found real hope!"

—**Brad Bigney,** lead pastor of Grace Fellowship in Florence, Kentucky, certified ACBC counselor and conference speaker, and author of *Gospel Treason: Betraying the Gospel with Hidden Idols*

"I spent nearly three decades of my life working with teens and young adults, and it's absolutely astonishing to me how much anxiety has spread in that age group over the last several years as a result of social media. It's practically an epidemic in our society, but it's hitting our kids the hardest—more than any generation that has come before. Josh's book reflects both what a great thinker he is and how well he understands people. If you or someone you love is struggling with anxiety, I cannot recommend anyone more highly than Josh Weidmann to help you take a biblical approach to dealing with it. It does not have to master you."

—**Curt Harlow**, senior pastor of Bayside Church in Sacramento, California

"As a person with an anxious imagination, I am grateful for Josh Weidmann's book *The End of Anxiety*. Josh does a great job of sharing his real struggle with anxiety, so he 'gets it.' Additionally, he bathes his thoughts in the truths and comforts of Scripture while giving tangible and practical applications that can be embraced by all of us anxious-type folks. Thank you, Josh!"

—**Mike Romberger**, president/CEO of Mount Hermon Christian Conference Center

"The anxiety woven into the fabric of every life requires careful investigation and biblical resolution. Josh Weidmann is a practitioner in the journey of coping with this common struggle. In *The End of Anxiety*, he shares transparently, insightfully, and wisely to provide the vital tools you need to embrace God's purposes and experience His liberating solutions."

—**Daniel Henderson**, president of Strategic Renewal International and author of *Transforming Prayer: How Everything Changes When You Seek God's Face*

THE END OF ANXIETY

THE END OF ANXIETY

THE END OF ANXIETY

THE BIBLICAL PRESCRIPTION FOR OVERCOMING FEAR, WORRY, AND PANIC

JOSH WEIDMANN

SALEM
BOOKS
an imprint of Regnery Publishing

Unless otherwise noted, all Scriptures are taken from THE HOLY BIBLE, ENGLISH STANDARD VERSION®. Copyright © 2001 by Crossway, a publishing ministry of Good News Publishers. Used by permission.

Scriptures marked KJV are taken from the KING JAMES VERSION, public domain.

Scriptures marked NASB are taken from the NEW AMERICAN STANDARD BIBLE®. Copyright © 1960, 1962, 1963, 1968, 1971, 1972, 1973, 1975, 1977, 1995 by the Lockman Foundation. Used by permission.

Scriptures marked NIV are taken from THE HOLY BIBLE, NEW INTERNATIONAL VERSION®. Copyright © 1973, 1978, 1984, 2011 by Biblica, Inc.™ Used by permission of Zondervan.

Scriptures marked NLT are taken from the HOLY BIBLE, NEW LIVING TRANSLATION. Copyright © 1996, 2004, 2007 by Tyndale House Foundation. Used by permission of Tyndale House Publishers, Inc., Carol Stream, Illinois, 60188. All rights reserved.

Scriptures marked TLB are taken from THE LIVING BIBLE. Copyright © 1971. Used by permission of Tyndale House Publishers, Inc., Carol Stream, Illinois, 60188. All rights reserved.

Published in Association with The Bindery Agency. www.TheBinderyAgency.com.

Salem Books™ is a trademark of Salem Communications Holding Corporation
Regnery® is a registered trademark of Salem Communications Holding Corporation

ISBN: 978-1-62157-973-1
eISBN: 978-1-62157-997-7

Library of Congress Control Number: 2020932935

Published in the United States by
Salem Books
An imprint of Regnery Publishing
A division of Salem Media Group
300 New Jersey Ave NW
Washington, DC 20001
www.SalemBooks.com

Manufactured in the United States of America

10 9 8 7 6 5 4 3 2 1

Books are available in quantity for promotional or premium use. For information on discounts and terms, please visit our website: www.Regnery.com.

For My Forever.

Molly, thank you for your endless and unconditional love.
What we have, no one can steal, replicate, or destroy.
I love you more with every passing day.
You know better than anyone
what this book has cost—
thank you for believing in me.
Thank you for never leaving my side
and for pointing me to Christ every single day.
I wouldn't want to do life and serve Jesus with anyone else.

SOS 3.4

I love you, babe.

CONTENTS

CORE PRINCIPLES

CHAPTER ONE: God has a purpose for all things in our lives, even anxiety. If the chief end of man is to glorify God, then we can trust that our anxiety is doing something for our good and God's glory.

CHAPTER TWO: Anxiety comes from a variety of sources. No matter its origin, God holds the outcome and offers hope for you through the journey.

CHAPTER THREE: Anxiety, fear, worry, and panic are triggers for greater dependence on God. Running from God when I cannot feel Him will result in forfeiting the peace He offers me in the darkest parts of my life.

CHAPTER FOUR: God created my emotions, and He invites me to process my feelings before Him so He can interact with me, calm me, and change me.

CHAPTER FIVE: Life is a marathon, not a sprint, and the sin of doubting God's sovereignty can weigh us down. It's our sacred responsibility to be honest about where our doubts and anxiety may lead us and build our foundation on our Savior and His Word.

CHAPTER SIX: When it comes to finding peace, we often look to counterfeit comforts. We look for things that will bring us momentary pleasure or ease our pain. The power of God offers joy and peace, no matter our emotions or circumstances.

CHAPTER SEVEN: While anxiety is deeply personal, it cannot be fought by ourselves. We must find the help we need through Christ in community, biblical counseling, and the Body of Christ to find inner peace.

CHAPTER EIGHT: God gives me hope and help to renew my mind when my thoughts get off track so that I never have to replay the same tracks again. Trusting God in times of turbulence demands that I cling to what is true. The Bible says, "Whatever is true, noble and right...think on such things" (Philippians 4:8).

CHAPTER NINE: It is possible to regain stability and find security, but it will only come by changing our motives, thinking, and behavior. Doing what you've been doing will only give you the same results.

CHAPTER TEN: There are two kinds of fear: (1) fear of God and (2) fear of reasonable danger. Both types of fear demand that we cultivate awe for God that compels us to run to Him, not away from Him.

CHAPTER ELEVEN: God's steadfast love for me is true even when He allows suffering in my life. The pain I am going through is making me more like Christ and securing my identity in Him.

CHAPTER TWELVE: Depression and anxiety are closely related and often experienced as a one-two punch to our hearts. Having the right perspective is essential for fighting and overcoming both through the power of Jesus and the peace of the Holy Spirit.

CHAPTER THIRTEEN: Dealing with anxiety demands that I find healing from Christ for my sin and begin healing from the hurt caused by others.

CHAPTER FOURTEEN: The antidote to anxiety is not sourced from our hearts. It can only come from the perfect peace found in Jesus, our Savior. No amount of "bootstrapping," self-help, or "I'll fix it myself" can compare to the peace of God that our hearts can barely comprehend.

CHAPTER FIFTEEN: I don't have to be anxious about being anxious ever again. Tomorrow has enough worries of its own, so I will focus on being bold and courageous today with the presence of Christ in my life.

CHAPTER SIXTEEN: Waiting upon the Lord means that I bind myself to Him and His purposes. It can give me the ultimate confidence and strength that can only come from His ever-present Spirit.

OVERTURE
MAKE IT STOP

"Am I crazy? Am I alone?"

My thumb hovered over the "send" button as my hands shook and my lips quivered. That night, I wanted to wave some sort of white flag surrendering myself to the wisdom of a close friend. Typing each letter felt like its own feat. I wanted to know that I was not alone or going mad—because both of those felt like reality to me. Doubt, disillusionment, anger, fear, sadness, and panic were plaguing my heart and perspective.

Anxiety was literally killing me. My sleep was gone. I couldn't eat. My head felt like it was going to explode, while my blood pressure plummeted. It was as if my heart was too weak to even pump. I would lay awake at night soaking my pillow with tears, longing for the anxiety to go away. I would repeatedly pray—no, *beg*— "God, please make it stop!"

I know good and well what it feels like when anxiety tries to kill you. If I am fully honest, there have been times when I wished it would take me out, just to get the pain to stop. I've paced the floor in the middle of the night. I've curled up in an empty bathroom stall, choking back tears and trying to keep my stomach from crawling out of my throat. I've told God that I thought it would be more merciful of Him to take my life than to leave me alive. You can imagine what this kind of anxiety did to my beautiful bride, Molly, and to my closest friends, who knew the real arena I was fighting in day in and day out.

My earliest memory of anxiety in my life, now looking back, is when I was called a "worry wart" as a kid. I seemed to easily get preoccupied with worst-case scenarios. The things I loved the most were the very things I was anxious about most often. Losing my family, losing my calling, even losing my salvation—these were all veins of thought that consumed my mind if I let them. I covered any anxiety by pushing my life to the max, overloading my schedule, accomplishing as much as possible, and keeping a sunshiny smile.

It wasn't until my adult years that I realized anxiety was more of a permanent resident in my life. It had claimed "squatter's rights" by simply hanging out for a long time and only causing a ruckus at a few poignant points along the way. For the most part, I just shunned the emotion, not giving it much thought or attention.

A few years ago, I went through my worst personal trial. The smile faded, the veneer of busyness was failing me, and my body was showing signs of physical stress. That, and the fact that my five-year-old daughter Gracie was acting just like I did at her age—anxious about everything—clued me in to the fact that anxiety was a *lifelong* squatter. One day, I was holding Gracie on the couch, and a wave of anxiety started crashing over me. Not wanting her to know it, but not able to keep it in, I audibly whispered, "*Lord Jesus, help!*" Gracie heard it, and later, in the midst of her own heightened anxiety, she asked Molly, "Mom, what is wrong with Dad?"

Later on, as Molly recounted our daughter's question and how it bothered her, I realized that anxiety was real in my life. But that was only the beginning. It was as if finally calling out this squatting emotion gave it all the more permission to invade and claim what it didn't rightfully own. Over the next few years, I experienced my fair share of crying sessions on my counselor's couch. I had many late-night or mid-Saturday-afternoon calls with my biblical counselor to help me just pull it together enough to be the pastor I needed to be the next morning or the dad I wanted to be to play catch with my son that afternoon.

Anxiety and depression are real emotions that God allows me to feel. I've begged Him to take both away, but they still seem to remain. No matter the eviction notices, they move right back in. I resolved that these emotions show me where I need to find Christ more in my life. I still placate my pain at times with a busy schedule. Yes, I still have my moments of tingling, sweaty palms or shortness of breath. But I've learned that a good, loving, and sovereign God allows these emotions in my life so I may be more dependent on Christ.

For the most part, my crutches are now removed, and the false gospels or coping mechanisms are replaced with a real love and dependence on Jesus. I cringe now when I hear people give anxiety advice like "Go squeeze an ice cube between your fingertips" or "Count your breaths for one minute." Those pieces of advice aren't going to help me find the end of anxiety. I'm allergic to false hope and faulty theology. If I don't have real help for my anxiety, then I know it will just keep coming back and wreaking havoc on my life. So please know that I will not use the pages of this book to build some kind of scaffolding around your life to try to prop up your mental health like an inevitable house of cards. Rather, I want you to realize that when you are broken into pieces on the Solid Rock of Jesus, the feelings that overwhelm you for a moment fade in the eternal light of His glory.

THE CAVEAT OF ALL CAVEATS: COULD THIS *REALLY* BE THE END OF YOUR ANXIETY?

In addition to being a man who has struggled with anxiety and seen God's help and hope through it, I am also a pastor and a certified biblical counselor. I have served in several pastoral roles in

Denver and Chicago, two of which have been as senior pastor. I am
currently the senior pastor of Grace Chapel in Denver, Colorado.

My primary passion is to apply the practical power of Jesus
Christ to everyday life. I do this by pastoring, preaching, writing,
and biblically counseling others. I have started two biblical counseling centers, including one that I currently oversee called the Hope
of Denver Biblical Counseling Center. We provide free counseling
to our church and our community because I want people to know
the power of Jesus to help them with any problem they may face.

The guidance you will find in this book will deal with the biblical prescription for anxiety, fear, worry, and panic. I am not a
medical doctor, but I do believe there is a role for doctors in our
lives. I believe the Bible has a lot to say about the whole person, not
just the soul, yet it may be right for you to seek the common grace
of medical advice and care for your outer self while we deal with
the deeper inner self (2 Corinthians 4:16). There may be a need for
you to deal with things chemically or physically, and I encourage
you to do so if that's appropriate—I just won't be addressing it
specifically in this book.

The truths of the Bible are not supposed to minimize or dismiss
the struggles we face. We do not reduce the Scriptures to be something like, "Take these Bible verses like Advil, get some rest, and
you'll be better by morning." Feelings of depression and anxiety
can and will haunt people for long seasons of life—or even an entire
life—but in our weakness, the power of God can be recognized as
a truly healing salve and not just a superficial cover-up.

I don't want this to disappoint or mislead you, so stick with me
for a second: The title of this book is a play on words. **Please know
that I don't assume you can find the end of your anxiety, but I do
believe we can find something better than simply making the madness stop.** The end of our anxiety is not merely the ceasing of it;
rather, it is finding the power of God within it. I am setting out on

this journey with you to prove my hypothesis, which is that *the end* or *the purpose* of our anxiety is to glorify God and enjoy Him forever. I do believe that you can enter into a sort of emotional and spiritual remission of anxiety if you apply the principles we will unpack along the way. However, I am not God, so I cannot promise it will ever be completely gone; it is only God's decision as to whether the thorn of our anxiety (or any suffering, for that matter) will ever be taken from us. But if we trust Him and grow in the likeness of His Son as we battle these emotions, we are indeed finding *God's end of anxiety.*

Anxiety is the great bully of our emotions. It pummels our soul and leaves us sapped of energy and hope. There's one truth it doesn't want us to entertain, let alone see for ourselves: **anxiety is a liar.** Even if anxiety tells you it will win, it won't. While it's a brutal bully, anxiety is still an emotion under the sovereign hand of God and never outside His control.

The seasons when anxiety has been the worst in my life are the seasons when I have allowed it to be the loudest. I will never forget being in a room with my biblical counselor, my dad, and an elder from our church. I didn't eat for days before that moment, and I had to keep a lozenge in my mouth just to keep it moist. I dreaded that day, and frankly, I hated that whole session. We were wading deep into the situation that had caused me the greatest panic when my biblical counselor said to me in the calmest voice possible, "I'm disappointed you did not run to God's Word first. You know better."

He was right—I did know better. I was running to a thousand other things to find comfort, but I wasn't allowing the Bible to be the security blanket of truth I so desperately needed. I knew the Bible would bring comfort. For crying out loud, I preached that principle over and over again! Yet that is where anxiety is a liar and a bully in my life. Keeping me from feasting on faith, it robs me of my joy and the courage that comes from the saving power of Christ, and it tells me that everything I know to be true is actually false.

The Psalmist David came to his senses at some point, shrugging off his anxiety and running to God for joy. He wrote in Psalm 94, "When anxiety was great within me, your consolation brought me joy" (Psalm 94:19 NIV). When I first started to deal with anxiety, I wish I could have said the same thing as the Psalmist. However, it wasn't until anxiety broke me for good that I realized the only way to conquer it was by leaning into the power of God's Word.

I have anxiety—or better said, anxiety has had me.

My prayers asking God to eradicate my anxiety for good have been frequent and repetitive. Just when I think I may have found the end of anxiety, it seems to pop back up like an evil clown, igniting chaos in my heart once again. It's clear that anxiety clings to me far more tightly than I would ever wish.

One morning, I was meeting a pastor friend of mine for breakfast. I had just finished telling him about my most recent bout of four long months of anxiety. As I finished, it was as if we were swapping big-fish stories. He chimed in, "You think that was bad...let me tell you about my anxiety a few years ago..." On his story went, and I realized a few things, two of which are worth mentioning:

(1) I am not alone.

(2) I am not crazy.

As he neared the end of his story and confessed that anxiety was a frequent visitor for him too, he stated, "I had to stop praying, 'God, make it stop.'" He paused before adding, "What if we are asking for the wrong thing—God, make it stop? Maybe that is the wrong prayer." He then went on to explain that "God, make it stop!" seems to be the most logical prayer for us to ask of a loving God. But what if God's will is to use the anxiety we face to make us more like Christ? He boldly asserted, "Josh, stop praying for

God to make it stop and start praying for God to make you more like Christ."

He was right—I had the end all wrong.

The end goal of all of this madness is to make me more like Christ. I need to pray for that end way more than I need to pray for my anxiety to end. I wanted my panic to cease, but perhaps I was defining the end by my terms, not God's terms. His purpose, even in my suffering, will always be better than simply a lack of suffering. I can endure all things, including paralyzing emotions or dramatic physical reactions, if I know that all of this will help me love God more and become more like His Son, Jesus Christ.

Anxiety may be a pesky, persistent pressure in your life, but what if you allowed your faith in God to be more relentless than any other overwhelming emotion?

In the end, my friend texted back: "You are not crazy. You are not alone. Isaiah 41:10, 'Fear not, for I am with you; be not dismayed, for I am your God; I will strengthen you, yes, I will help you, I will uphold you with my righteous right hand.'"

So now it is my turn to say to you: **You are not alone. You are not crazy.** Let's go find God's chief end for anxiety. We are on this journey together.

—Josh Weidmann

WHAT IS THE PURPOSE OF ANXIETY?

CHAPTER 1

THE CHIEF END OF EVERYTHING

START WITH SCRIPTURE
Romans 11:36; 1 Corinthians 10:31; Psalm 73:25

CORE PRINCIPLE ONE

God has a purpose for all things in our lives, even anxiety. If the chief end of man is to glorify God, then we can trust that our anxiety is doing something for our good and God's glory.

D owntown Chicago. Middle of the night. Just a kid in his twenties.
My producer and I had just finished recording on Chicago's WMBI radio station. That was the best time to record—during his late-night shift. After wrapping up our work, we shared a few laughs, said our goodbyes, and I caught the last train from Union Station to my suburban apartment.

I remember little of anything after the conductor punched my ticket. I was exhausted, slouching, and soon sound asleep. The train had a way of rocking me to la-la land as if I were an infant back in my mother's arms. Trains do that sometimes.

Honestly, that train ride might have been some of the best sleep of my life...until the conductor's voice shook apart my slumber.

"Son, you've got to get off. Last stop."

My eyes snapped awake, and I frantically found my bearings. Nothing looked familiar. This wasn't my stop. Not even close. That's when I saw the name of the station. It was nowhere near my home.

Two questions raced to the front of my mind: *Where am I? How did I get here?*

How I got there was obvious—a bit of REM sleep combined with a racing train will eventually take you anywhere you never intended to be.

When I realized where I was, I was stuck in a state of confusion and quickly rising panic. I knew I was on the last train of the night. I had slept until the end of the line and missed my stop by miles. There weren't any more trains running for at least five hours. Oh, and did I mention it was winter outside?

As the train came to its usual screeching halt, I looked frantically for the conductor. He was standing outside the door a few cars down.

"Sir, I missed my stop back at Palatine. What should I do now?"

What did I expect him to say? Maybe I thought he would say, "No problem, son, I'll whip this train around, and we'll take you back." Not even close.

His cold reply still sticks in my mind: "The next train headed that way is at 5:47 a.m."

No "I'm sorry to hear that…good luck…stay warm…" Nothing. Just a simple train schedule as factual and cold as the one hanging on the wall behind him.

After standing at that station for a few minutes—still half asleep, confused, and, frankly, lost—I realized I had no choice but to walk home. I followed the tracks, figuring I would either make it home before the train started again, it would pick me up on its first run...or the conductor would feel some remorse when he passed my frozen corpse in the morning.

I found myself on a journey that was unplanned, uncertain, and unwelcome.

WHAT TRACK AM I ON... AND WHAT'S MY DESTINATION RIGHT NOW?

Anxiety can feel a lot like a late-night train ride to nowhere. As we grapple with overwhelming emotions, we can question the purpose of our struggle and the end goal of all this chaos.

As a follower of Jesus, I believe all things work together for my good and God's glory. But to be honest, when I contrast that truth with my anxiety, worry, and panic, I don't find comfort. If God's supremely in control, then why does He allow anxiety to invade my heart? Doesn't He care? Doesn't He see that I'm headed toward the wrong destination, facing a bitterly cold journey back to the warmth of home?

Doesn't it sometimes seem like His response is as cold and indifferent as the conductor's? It can be confusing at best how a good God would allow this chaotic emotional state to hijack my journey. That doesn't sound like a *good* God at all.

A gathering of Puritans wrote the *Westminster Shorter Catechism* in the 1600s. They took the thirty-nine articles of the *Westminster Confession* and reframed them into a more specific set of doctrines meant to be easily understood and accessible to all.

The shorter catechism comprised of 107 questions and answers was designed to educate everyday people in matters of doctrine and unbelief. The first question of the *Westminster Shorter Catechism* asks, "What is the chief end of man?" This is probing.

If we are honest, we have all asked this question before, but probably not with those same words. We may ask questions like: *Why am I alive? What is my purpose? Where is this thing headed?*

The shorter catechism answers the question by stating, "Man's chief end is to glorify God and fully enjoy Him forever."

If the end of the line for us is to glorify God forever, then can we safely assume every emotion and stop along the way is helping us awaken our purpose? Is it possible that even our anxiety—that throat-constricting, pulse-racing, headache-inducing, feet-freezing grip on our hearts—is *allowed* into our lives to help us know our purpose?

When I began to write this book, I wanted to discover a way to make my anxiety end. *Begone from me, you evil feelings!* I wanted to know if there was a purpose behind my pain. Instead, my search for anxiety's end led me to discover a different kind of end...the end that God designed far before my existence.

I was very familiar with the *Westminster Shorter Catechism.* I knew that the chief end of all things was for me to bring glory to God and enjoy Him forever, including celebrating Him through my emotions. But how could that possibly be true for my anxiety?

The purpose, the goal, the chief end of my anxiety is to bring God glory. While that doesn't exactly feel like a cup of Chicken Soup for the Soul, there is some comfort that comes in knowing that God has a purpose in my pain.

I've accepted that I may never find the true end of my anxiety. It comes in waves, ebbing and flowing, sometimes worse than others. I know there may still be tsunamis of anxiety cresting over me, but I can rest assured that God is working out His intentions. Even amid anxious feelings, I can trust Him completely. I must strive to use my worry, depression, panic, and fear to drive me to glorify God even more.

We find the secret to bringing glory at the end of the statement "enjoy Him forever."

We glorify God by finding joy in the Lord amidst the pain and pleasures of life. When you're sitting in the ashes and rubble of your life, surrounded by the smoldering embers of your decisions or whatever life threw your way, even though hope seems lost, there can be peace in knowing all of this is for some greater purpose. When we find joy couched in suffering, we are on the path to fulfilling our chief end. Finding the end of anxiety begins with trusting that God's chief end is best.

JOY FLOWS FROM FAITH

"Joyful" is not a word I would use to describe my anxiety. We define joy as great pleasure, happiness, even fulfillment—not at all how it feels when you're in the grip of anxiety. That's not the prevailing feeling when my stomach lodges itself in my throat and my heart is beating out of my chest. However, the Bible seems to convey that we can have joy and should have joy always and forever (Psalm 145).

In times of great anxiety (or any other circumstance), sometimes the feeling of great pleasure and happiness can be difficult to find. But when I am in a panic, I can still have joy because joy is a state of mind, not a state of emotion.

I can have joy even if I don't have happiness. I can have joy even if I don't have peace. Why? Joy flows from faith and relying on God—no matter my circumstances. John Piper defines Christian joy as "a good feeling in the soul, produced by the Holy Spirit, as He causes us to see the beauty of Christ in the Word and in the world." Two elements are critical here. First, true joy is produced only by the Holy Spirit. Second, joy leads us to see the beauty of Christ in our broken world.

At the end of the day, joy is a shift in perspective, not a change in circumstances.

We can look at biblical examples like Job's suffering or Joseph's time at the bottom of the well and in a prison cell and observe how right suffering can lead to greater joy. Their circumstances didn't change; their perspectives did. Paul was quick to point out that we can have joy during our suffering, and he encouraged us to rejoice in the Lord always (Philippians 3:1, 4:4). To rejoice is to renew joy, no matter the situation we find ourselves in. Rejoicing is an intentional act to inspire our soul with greater confidence and trust in God. The very fact that our joy needs renewal means that it can and will be depleted. But with the help of God, we can reinvigorate our souls with faith and trust in Him, even when circumstances or emotions don't change.

When my focus is on God's purposes and not my problems, the endgame changes. My joy comes not by the relieving of my anxiety, but by seeing how God is working in my anxiety. David Powlison said it well: "God wants us to know Him so intimately and trust Him so completely that our desire to fix our troubles in our own way will no longer consume us."

God may not make all your anxiety go away, but He can cultivate in you a heart of trust toward Him that will help you have a deep sense of joy in spite of the circumstances and emotions you are feeling.

I SAW THE END . . . AND I LIKED IT

I can remember going home from the hospital at 2:00 a.m. after one of my worst panic attacks. I got back into my bed only to wrestle with demons and crazy feelings until dawn. I thought I would die that night. The emotions and spiritual attacks are memories I hate to even recall. At one point, I laid my head in the depths of my pillow and started screaming out to the Lord, *"Make it stop! Make it stop! Please, Lord, make it stop!"*

Eventually, the anxiety subsided, and peace returned. I can't say I ever truly found the end of anxiety, but God found me and showed me His chief end in my anxiety.

I remember lying in my bed that Saturday and having a sense of joy. It was as if God were saying to me, "Though this anxiety may never end, I am in charge of its purpose." He was working out something in me that could not be worked out otherwise. That day, my marriage grew stronger, the love for my kids grew deeper, and my dependence upon Christ grew even more steadfast.

During one of the worst hours of begging the Lord through my tears to make it stop, my faithful friend Jason showed up at our house. With my wife lying on one side of me, he came and lay on the other side, gripping my hand with all his strength as I clung to his arm for dear life. Back and forth, Jason and Molly prayed for me, asking God to make it stop.

God used Jason and Molly to help me find purpose and joy in the pain. Did we find the end of anxiety? No, but they helped me find God, who holds the end purpose in the palm of His hand. I saw the end goal that God had in mind, and I found joy in it.

To avoid God's chief end for all mankind—including in our emotions—will only fuel our anxiety more. We are for Him or against Him; there is no middle ground here (Deuteronomy 28:47). Anxiety is often fueled by our lack of trust in God. Anxiety will eat your faith for lunch if you let it—but the more we lean into the end goal of God's glory, the more anxiety's strength and presence will fade.

The first key to using our spiritual identity to calm our anxiety is this: abide in God by embracing Jesus as Lord. If you will use your anxiety to strengthen your trust in our Mighty Savior, not only will you find the end of anxiety, but you will also find joy in Him along the journey. This results from pleasing God; He rewards those who seek Him (Hebrews 11:6).

THE END OF THE LINE WILL EVENTUALLY LEAD YOU HOME

That night when I fell asleep on the train and found myself at the end of the line, it felt like I had unexpectedly ended up on a ride to nowhere. As I started walking in the dark, I thought I would freeze before ever finding the warmth of home again. Yet as I walked along the rail line that night, I came across a glowing gas station with an on-duty police officer inside. I stepped in to get warm, only to have the officer ask me why I was walking in the middle of the night. I told him I had fallen asleep and ended up far from home. He graciously said, "Get in the car. I'll take you home."

Anxiety is like that: the journey is never something you would choose, but God has blessings to show you along the way. You may never find the end of anxiety, but you can find God's end in it. Weeping may stay the night, but joy comes in the morning (Psalm 30:5).

THREE STEPS TOWARD THE END OF ANXIETY

ACT

Make a list of ten to twenty things you think God may be developing in you through this season of anxiety. Carry the list with you for the next week, reflecting on it and why a good, all-powerful God would allow you to go through this season. Then share your list with a friend.

PRAY

Spend some undistracted time in prayer asking God to show you what true joy looks like in your current circumstances.

MEMORIZE

Philippians 4:4: "Rejoice in the Lord always; again I will say, rejoice."

CHAPTER 2

AFRAID FOR NOTHING

START WITH SCRIPTURE
Psalm 118:6; Philippians 4:6–7

CORE PRINCIPLE TWO
Anxiety comes from a variety of sources. No matter its origin,
God holds the outcome and offers hope for you through the journey.

Cancer is never fair, but it seems especially cruel when it strikes a child. Two-year-old David was taken by his mother, Deborah, to Massachusetts General Hospital in Boston, where they met with Dr. John Truman, a specialist in treating children with cancer and various blood diseases. Dr. Truman's leukemia prognosis was devastating: "David has a fifty-fifty chance of survival."

Countless clinic visits followed filled with blood tests, scans, shots, and intravenous drugs. Through it all, David never cried in the waiting room or on the way to the doctor's office. Although his new friends at the clinic needed to stick him with needles and administer painful treatments, David hustled in ahead of his mother with a smile, excited by the celebrity-level welcome he always received from the nursing staff.

When he was three, David endured a spinal tap—an excruciating procedure at any age. His mom explained to him that because he was sick, Dr. Truman had to help him get better. "If it hurts, remember it's because he loves you." The procedure was horrendous. It took three nurses to hold David still while he yelled and sobbed and struggled. When it was almost over, the tiny boy, soaked in sweat and tears, looked up at the doctor and gasped, "Thank you, Dr. Tooman, for my hurting."

Facing trials takes the faith of a child and the courage of a lion. Whether they come by our own hand or through circumstances allowed by God and beyond our control, it's easy to flinch at the pain and rarely turn around and say, "Thank you, Lord, for allowing my pain." However, both the apostles Paul and Peter said we find our true character by trials (Romans 4, James 1). Our trust in God is tested when we experience the pressure of stress, anxiety, and chaos. James 1:3 reminds us, "For you know that when your faith is tested, your endurance has a chance to grow" (NLT).

You are likely facing a trial now that you'd rather avoid. If you're not currently facing a hardship, I'm sure you have faced one in the past or will face one in the future. Life is full of circumstances where our stamina is tested and our faith is stretched. In these trials, it's human nature to bury ourselves in anxiety, worry, and depression, wondering how and if we will ever get through what we're facing.

It can feel like God is either nowhere to be found or standing over us like a schoolteacher waiting to see if we will make it through the test. If God is a God of peace, grace, and love, it can be confusing as to why we feel uneasy in our souls.

CAUSES OF ANXIETY

There is no shortage of situations that threaten to overwhelm us in this world. We can experience anxiety in any one of these four categories, each of which can have dozens of different applications:

1. Spiritual issues. Anxiety can come during the battle with our flesh—our sinful desires and actions (Romans 7:19). This battle most certainly can relate to sin that we have yet to repent of or confess (1 John 1:9; James 5:16), but it can also relate to past sin that has been dealt with but which still is bearing consequences in our lives.

Anxiety can also come from spiritual warfare as our unseen enemy battles against us. Our battle is not just against flesh and blood, but against rulers and those with influence and dominion in the demonic realm (Ephesians 6:12).

Anxiety will also spike up for some who know God is asking them to do something they don't want to do—take Jonah, for example, in the Old Testament. He ran to Joppa to get away from God's calling to go preach in Tarshish (Jonah 1). Or take Ananias in the New Testament, who was asked by God to go meet with the Christian-hater Saul (who later became Paul); he asked a few anxious questions of God to make sure He had chosen the right guy (Acts 9:13).

Anxiety can come from not having salvation in Jesus Christ. Without Christ, our minds are dark, and our hearts are veiled. Romans 1:20–21 tells us that we can be aware of God's common grace, but our minds are "futile" and "darkened" by sin in the world. It is only by the redeeming power of Christ that people can have the veil lifted from their minds and hearts and be able to see God as He is, subsequently showing them their need for Him (2 Corinthians 3:14–15).

2. Bodily issues. We as humans are made of two parts—a material part and an immaterial part. There are biological and organic issues that can be cared for by those who deal only with the physical aspects of humans. The roles of doctors, medicine, and surgery are necessary to care for the physical being. We are grateful for the common grace of knowledge and medical advancements that allow man to know how to care for physical needs.

Our souls do have a sort of independence from our bodies (1 Corinthians 14:14; Romans 8:16), but it is only removed from our physical bodies when we die. While we are alive, these two elements do not act entirely independently; the whole person—body and soul—is in need of help and redemption.

When dealing with the physical aspects of anxiety, there can be a place for medical doctors to help people with their bodies. Sometimes, there is a physical issue with the mind (lack of sleep, nutrition, hormones, and so forth) that needs to be addressed by a doctor. However, there can also be issues of the soul (worry, anxiety, fear, etc.) that can be transformed by the power of God's Word. There is overlap here; body and soul are combined to produce a single entity. The Word of God is sufficient to help the whole person, yet there may be a need to submit ourselves to the care of those who can help us with our outer self as we seek to find strength in the inner self (2 Corinthians 4:16).

In this book, I am going to be far more focused on the spiritual side of anxiety. While this effort may help you with your physical symptoms, it may be necessary to find a medical professional to help you with any bodily afflictions you may be experiencing.

3. Relational issues. Relationships are not always smooth sailing, nor should we expect them to be. We are sinful, broken people who are trying to live at peace with other sinful, broken people. Marital problems, singleness, friendships, family members, co-working relationships, abusive relationships, or guilt and shame for what was said or done long ago to hurt someone—all of these can produce significant anxiety. Especially if you are a person who longs to please other people, or if you live to be a peacemaker, the second your relationships are void of perfect harmony, anxiety comes screeching in.

Anxiety can also come when those we love are hurting or battling their own physical or spiritual issues. We can have anxiety over a wayward child or a parent battling cancer.

4. Circumstantial issues. Deadlines, employment (or lack thereof), responsibilities, the unknown, failure, and making mistakes can cause us to be anxious. We can worry over plans and desires for the *future* circumstances: social status, measuring up, doing something meaningful or ambitious, and receiving praise or notoriety. Still others are lost in a season of depression over *present* circumstances: feelings of despondency, dread, or deep pain caused by missed opportunities, a broken promise, or a financial crisis.

Anxiety can also manifest as stress over circumstances. It could be that we are anxious that our to-do list is too full or that a room is too crowded. My friend Matt can be paralyzed at the thought of being called on to speak in front of other people—so much so that he lies awake for days before a meeting or social event. That doesn't seem to be a problem for me, but give me a few missed deadlines or too much to get done in a day and my anxiety spills over.

Other circumstances like not eating, not eating well, caffeine consumption, alcohol misuse, and not sleeping will cause chaos for us. Also, personal triggers that bring back bad memories when we find ourselves in a new setting can cause a person's heart to race, blood pleasure to rise, and shortness of breath.

GOD, IS THIS A TEST?

No matter which of these four categories we find ourselves experiencing, we likely will ask the question: "God, is this a test?"

This question is natural for those of us who are trying to figure out why God would allow us to experience anxiety, worry, or depression.

I hate tests. I always have. In high school, I was so terrified of tests that I arranged a time to take them apart from the rest of the class. Often, I would be issued the test and then go to the principal's office to take it. I would sit by myself without anyone there to make me tense—or conversely, so I would not distract others with my bouncing leg or tapping pencil. I still disdain tests to this day, and I am not just talking about fill-in-the-bubble or essay sorts of tests. I don't like feeling that I'm being evaluated.

Yet it only makes sense that God has the right to test me. There is no reason why He can't look into my mind, which He created, or my heart, which He also created, and perceive the angst inside. I don't have to be afraid of God's testing of my heart; rather, I should welcome the chance to be intimately known by Him.

One particular night depicted in the New Testament could easily be overlooked by a careless reader, but it was not something the disciples would soon forget. This story unfolds in just a few verses in the gospels of Matthew, Mark, and John, coming right after the more memorable event of Jesus's feeding five thousand people. According to Mark, tensions in the crowd were growing. John tells us that Jesus knew they were about to take Him by force (John 6:15), so He told His disciples to leave without Him:

> Immediately he made the disciples get into the boat and go before him to the other side, while he dismissed the crowds. And after he had dismissed the crowds, he went up on the mountain by himself to pray. When evening came, he was there alone, but the boat by this time was a long way from the land, beaten by the waves, for the

wind was against them. And in the fourth watch of the night he came to them, walking on the sea. But when the disciples saw him walking on the sea, they were terrified, and said, "It is a ghost!" and they cried out in fear. But immediately Jesus spoke to them, saying, "Take heart; it is I. Do not be afraid" (Matthew 14:22–27).

Evening came, but Jesus still hadn't come. Jesus had told them to cross the Sea of Galilee (in Mark), but John's writings capture the raw emotion of the moment when they had to decide to move on *without* Jesus. I imagine they waited as long as they could. They probably even debated among themselves, asking, "Are you sure we should go without Jesus?" These men had left their jobs, families, and lives to follow Him. Now they were going to embark without Him.

Fear and anxiety had to be setting in for them at the thought. What if we never find Him? What if something happens to Him—or us?

They started rowing across to Capernaum. I imagine they stayed as close to shore as possible, hoping to pick up Jesus along the route. But it wasn't working out that way. The wind drove them further and further south—so much so that they lost sight of the shore and relinquished the hope of picking up Jesus. Matthew is graphic in describing the effects of this storm, saying the boat was literally being tormented. The storm raged, the waves crashed, and the wind pummeled the ship.

As fear, doubt, and anxiety set in, they must have wondered if Jesus had forgotten them. After all, Jesus had sent them out there, so He had to have known this was going to happen. Imagine the fearful thoughts that must have gripped their hearts: *Did Jesus forget about us? Did Jesus just not care? Things look really bad—how will it end?*

If these thoughts sound familiar to you, you are not alone. I've thought those words. I've felt my heart clenched in the talons of those thoughts. When the storms of life are pummeling our hearts and minds, it's easy to let doubts hijack our perspective.

Some of our greatest times of doubt come when Jesus pulls away from us (or when we perceive that He does). When we cannot see or hear Him, we begin to question His care. Our normal reaction in the midst of a storm is to freak out (anxiety), forget our faith (worry), and run to false comforts (depression). But what if God sends us into the storms, knowing that these trials will develop in us a deeper longing for Him?

What happened next to the disciples is astounding. The waves grew out of control, and the absence of Christ grew more alarming. And then...they saw something. Matthew said, "But when the disciples saw him walking on the sea, they were terrified, and said, 'It is a ghost!' and they cried out in fear." The disciples feared the darkness, the rough waters, and the way that Jesus was showing up to meet them.

Going out on the water in darkness was not normal or natural. The rough seas also provided unnatural conditions for sailing. Every good Galilean fisherman knew to stay on shore if a storm was brewing. Yet they did as Jesus told them. John mentions that they had gone only about three or four miles, making the point that they were not moving far or fast. The sea was against them, and they were understandably afraid. All the while, Jesus knew they were going to be tested in this way.

Anxiety was the disciples' natural reaction in unnatural circumstances. Not only was sailing in the darkness and rough water unusual, but what they saw next was even more unnatural—it was *supernatural*, and they were terrified.

To fear sailing in darkness and through rough waters is not surprising, but why did they fear Jesus? Because He was "walking on the sea." The disciples probably assumed that they were seeing a spirit. During the time when this story took place, there was a superstition that "night spirits"—such as the Greek goddess Nyx—came out in the dark. If these spirits materialized on the sea, they were thought to be manifestations of people who had died in the water.

But what the disciples saw was not a dead man or the spirit of a dead man; this was the God-Man. The Prince of Peace Himself brought anxiety to the disciples' hearts. Knowing their fear, Jesus walked toward them—*on water.* Their first instinct was to believe this was a spirit or ghost, not Christ. So they let their imaginations run wild.

We often have the same response. We allow our fears to mushroom and metastasize within our imagination. The fears frequently are not based on reality—they're only speculation that turns into suspicion before we start obsessing about what could happen next. God can calm our imagined fears, but He is often far more concerned about real-world troubles than engaging in "What if?" mind games. As Charles Spurgeon said, "The rod of God does not smite us as sharply as the rod of our own imagination."

Making sense of our emotions requires reliance on God's power. While fear and anxiety are emotions God created, they are not emotions He wants to hijack our hearts. In 2 Timothy 1:6–7, the Apostle Paul wrote to his anxiety-stricken disciple Timothy, "I want to remind you to stir into flame the strength and boldness that is in you.... For the Holy Spirit, God's gift, does not want you to be afraid" (TLB). That passage goes on to say that we are to have a spirit of "power and love and of a sound mind" (KJV).

Facing the fears in your life with the power of God can shrink them into manageable sizes or make them disappear altogether. Nothing is stronger than God's power—no emotion, no sickness, no circumstances, not even death. God's Word assures us that:

- He is more powerful than any demonic power (Matthew 12:28)
- He is the Creator of all life (John 6:63; Romans 8:11)
- He gives you strength to live out His plan for you (1 Corinthians 12:4)
- He can transform your life from dead in sin to alive in Him (Romans 12:1–2)

While smooth sailing is enjoyable, it has never been my most vibrant time of spiritual growth. When fear increases and my faith is tested, I grow in my longing for and reliance upon Jesus. Paul told Timothy not to be afraid and to embrace *power, love,* and a *sound mind.* At first glance, "a sound mind" may seem like an odd addition to *power* and *love,* but it is profound. A clear, focused, and trusting mind will not flutter from one fear to the next, dreaming up all that could go wrong. Rather, a sound mind is quick to take every thought captive, returning to the truth that God is sovereign, loving, and wise.

A sound mind sees anxious moments as an opportunity to seek Christ. When the disciples saw Jesus walking on the water, they had a choice: Would they be fearful at the appearance of Jesus, or would they rejoice in His presence? They did choose to rejoice, but not until Jesus said to them, "Take heart; it is I. Do not be afraid" (v. 27). Then they were glad to take Him into the boat, after which they immediately arrived at the place they were going.

Once they heard the voice of Jesus and saw His face, their fears subsided. Their story of fear ends with peace and points to our own situation. In the midst of our storms, do we keep rowing and rowing, thrashing about in our own imagination and impatience, fighting against the winds and waves of our fears? And when Jesus arrives—and He always shows up—do we welcome Him into the boat or fear Him and keep on rowing futilely in our own strength?

The disciples discovered the reality of Hebrews 7:25: "He is able also to save forever those who draw near to God through Him" (NASB). Faith is at the center of our choice to draw near or not. Feelings of fear and anxiousness are normal—but overwhelming and terrifying fear need not be. Our choice is whether we will "take Jesus in" or remain in fear. The antidote to fear is faith in Christ. The nineteenth-century German evangelist George Müller once said, "The beginning of anxiety is the end of faith. The beginning of true faith is the end of anxiety."

Of all the commands in the Bible, this one appears the most: "Do not be afraid." More than three hundred times God instructs His people not to be afraid. You might interpret this command as saying, "*Stop it right now! Just get over your fear already!*" You could see this as the Lord's yelling at you for doing something wrong. However, that would be a gross, callous misinterpretation of God's heart. God's command to "not be afraid" emanates from a Father's loving care and concern for His children.

No doubt you've heard a parent say to a child, "Be careful!" Technically, the mom or dad is giving a command, but the child doesn't take it that way. That's because the words spring from a nurturing, tender heart. Infused in that admonition to "be careful" is this sentiment: "I love you and want you to be safe." Jesus speaks with the same tenderness to us in our fear and worry—"Fear not," for My love for you is strong and caring as I want only what comes from the Father's goodness toward you (Luke 12:32). Paul David Tripp said, "I want the [anxious] person to remember that God is near, that He is present, that His grace reaches to the depth of those struggles—rather than 'if you do this, this, and this, you can become unanxious.'"[1]

FEAR NOT

In the midst of your storm with the waves crashing around you, are you struggling to hear God's voice? Are you allowing your imagination to run rampant? Are you fearful over what *could be* more than what actually *is*? Are you asking God to speak to you about something that exists only in your mind?

When your emotions rage on, do you doubt that Jesus is in the storm with you? He might have been silent for a while, but He has been walking alongside you. In His perfect timing, He will finally utter these comforting words: "It is I; do not be afraid." Our challenge—and opportunity—is to invite Him into our boat and let Him lead us to the solid ground of a safe harbor.

THREE STEPS TOWARD THE END OF ANXIETY

REFLECT

Keep a journal of when you feel fearful. Write down the date, time, circumstance, and what you were thinking and saying to yourself at that time. Evaluate what needs to be renewed in your thinking to avoid fear in the future (Romans 12:1–2).

READ

Study Psalm 56:3–4 in three different translations and ask God to make this passage a reality in your life.

DISCUSS

Find a trusted person in your life with whom you can talk about your fears and ask them to help you believe what is true and what may be mostly in your imagination.

CHAPTER 3

LEARNING TO TRUST GOD'S HEART WHEN I CAN'T FEEL HIS HAND

START WITH SCRIPTURE
Psalm 37:1–7; John 6:66–69

CORE PRINCIPLE THREE

Anxiety, fear, worry, and panic are triggers for greater dependence on God. Running from God when I cannot feel Him will result in forfeiting the peace He offers me in the darkest parts of my life.

Anger is a real feeling created by God. As the aircraft carrier in the fleet of our emotions, anger is massive, and a multitude of other feelings fly from it: grief, hatred, bitterness, sadness, horror, and doubt. Anger left alone will grow into something that can destroy us; anger correctly expressed to God can be a great tool for growing our spiritual maturity. Anger is something many individuals in the Bible experienced, including God Himself.

Anger is never stagnant; it is either growing or dying. When we are dissatisfied with God because of a situation or an unfulfilled expectation, the seeds of self-centeredness are planted. Our selfish hearts scream, *"I deserve better!"*—and this entitlement feeds our anger. If we allow this pride to grow, it can turn into a mighty oak of emotions with a root system reaching far into every area of our spiritual lives.

Conversely, if we are quick to deal with arrogance properly, the seeds soon die off, leaving the fresh soil of our souls ready to be planted with godly emotions such as love, joy, peace, patience, and kindness.

There are two kinds of anger toward God.

The first is unbelieving anger. This stems from a heart that does not trust God and refuses to believe His character is true. This kind of anger denies God is in control because, after all, if He were (we assume), He would have stopped our suffering. Unbelieving anger can move us to cynicism, looking for what's wrong in every situation, and distrusting any authority—especially spiritual authority.

Unbelieving anger is an attempt to break the relationship with God merely because a person has been hurt. Unbelieving anger tempts us to seal ourselves off in silence or distance from God and others to prevent more pain in this God-controlled world. Anger becomes sin when we use it to reject God's loving purpose and plan and resolve to remain embittered toward Him. Unbelief can render a person stone-deaf to God's voice and stone-hearted toward His people.

The second kind of anger is believing anger. This anger is expressed properly and not acted upon in sinful ways. It drives us to trust God's loving intentions even when we can't make sense of His actions. People who are angry at God while still trusting in His sovereignty allow their anger to move them to a place of greater surrender. They trust what they know about God, His character, and His purposes. They understand His attributes as more real and dependable than the emotions that overwhelm them. Anger is not sinful if it is biblically rooted, righteously processed, and leads us to believe God all the more.

Take Job as an example. He endured more than a few bad days in a row. Once a wealthy landowner, Job lost everything and everyone who was precious to him, all under the oversight—and with the permission—of God. When Job became increasingly angry, His friend Bildad recognized his struggle and responded, "You who tear yourself [up] in anger..." (Job 18:4). Job himself spoke with a depressed tone, frustrated at God's seeming lack of action, and said, "I cry to you for help and you do not answer me; I stand, and you only look at me. You have turned cruel to me..." (Job 30:20–21). Job expressed his anger *straight to God.*

However, God did not condemn Job for his anger; rather, God interacted with Job in his anger to teach and develop him. God convinced Job of His almighty power, His care for His creation, and His control over every situation. God used Job's questioning to deepen his belief and lead him into a greater surrender to God's power. The process for Job was like this:

- Job suffered: anxiety, worry, loss, fear, depression
- Job felt angry
- Job expressed his anger toward God in questioning and wrestling
- Job saw who God was and was reminded of His character
- Job surrendered to God's will

The truth is this: Like Job, at one time or another, all of us will wrestle with God—even though it never seems to be a fair fight. We struggle, kick, and push back. But when we wrestle with God, we find His hold on us to be much tighter than our hold on Him. His is the grip of a loving Father.

Job found this out the hard way. After Job was exhausted from wrestling, God asked him directly, "Shall a *faultfinder* contend with *the Almighty*? He who argues with God, let him answer it" (Job 40:2). Job the faultfinder remained silent. His anger was overthrown by God's almighty, perfect love.

My friend, resentment toward God will leave us empty-handed every time. We can keep our hands clenched like a fist in hostility, or we can open our palms in surrender to His Majesty.

THE GOD WHO OVERTHROWS

One of the best-known names for God is *El Shaddai*, which is often translated into English as "God Almighty." The Bible frequently borrows words from the surrounding cultures of its day and redeems their meanings. In the ancient Hebrew culture, the root word *Shadad* may have carried the idea of "the Thunderer" and was used to describe powerful weather patterns.

Another name for God, *Elohim*, refers to God as the Creator. But *Shaddai* is different from *Creator*; it carries the idea of the one who has ongoing control over nature and can make it do what is *contrary* to itself. When used as a name for God, *Shaddai* means that He is able to triumph over all obstacles and overcome all opposition. As a result, this name for God is used to describe God's power. *El Shaddai* can also be translated as "the Overpowerer," calling attention to the Lord's unmatched ability to do whatever He purposes to do (Exodus 15:6; Matthew 19:26). It also suggests the idea that God *overpowers us*. For some, this is a difficult and perhaps even offensive description. However, God's overpowering work always refers to His desire for us to become His and His alone.

While I may grow angry at God from time to time, I must always remember that He is not my enemy. He is my loving and powerful Father.

One of my favorite childhood memories is wrestling with my tall, muscular dad on the family room floor along with my three siblings. When I wrestle with God, the feelings remind me of those times. I'm like a child wrestling with his father—knowing that when He finally pins me to the shag carpet, He will then lean down while smiling and laughing and kiss my face. The One Who kisses my face is *El Shaddai*, the Overpowerer.

Such is the love of the Thunderer. The Almighty Father loves us and won't share us with another. Nothing on earth, not even a powerful emotion, will overthrow the desire God has to keep us as His own. If we allow our hearts to go on in anger, we will find ourselves worshipping at the altar of our emotions and not in the loving arms of God.

WHO ARE YOU WRESTLING WITH?

The late Jamie Buckingham tells this story:

> There was once a young apprentice who went to stay on an island with an elderly priest.
>
> One afternoon the young cleric, eager to learn, walked with the venerable man along the craggy shore. As their robes swirled in the wind, he finally asked his big question. "Father, do you still wrestle with the devil?"
>
> "No, my son," the elderly man answered, stroking his white beard. "I have grown old, and the devil has grown old with me. He does not bother me as before. Now I wrestle with God."
>
> "Wrestle with God? Do you hope to win?"
>
> The wrinkled old man looked his young consort in the eye.
>
> "Oh, no! I hope to lose."[1]

That is a powerful statement! The only person who would ever hope to lose to God is the person who understands that *El Shaddai* is the One he is wrestling. This is the beauty of spiritual surrender: we *stop* wrestling so God may become fully ours and we may become fully His.

Buckingham goes on to write, "Unfortunately, most of us seldom get to that place in life. We spend our years battling with Satan. The devil, however, is not man's real adversary—God is."[2]

When God overpowers us, He also seeks to overpower what dominates and rules our hearts in His place. He unseats those idols holding our hearts in bondage. Simultaneously, He unbinds our human loyalties from sin to then rebind us to Himself in an exclusive relationship.

When the *El Shaddai* becomes your *El Shaddai*, nothing is left to love more than Him, and there is nothing to fear because of Him. Anxieties decrease when you draw near to Him. No longer does anger overpower you for long periods of time; instead, your life is marked by the peaceful presence of the God who overthrows your emotions. Why? Because your feelings will fade in comparison to His blazing glory and the sweetness of His almighty love.

When we become desperate enough to be freed from our burdens, worries, anxieties, and fears, we cry out to God, asking Him to become our only true love and the only One we fear. When our own devices, plots, and human stumblings finally fail, we beg that He alone be our vision, destination, and passion.

Charles Spurgeon, the prince of preachers, arrived at this same conclusion in his own fight:

> While I regarded God as a tyrant, I thought my sin a
> trifle; but when I knew Him to be my Father, then I

mourned that I could ever have kicked against Him. When I thought God was hard, I found it easy to sin; but when I found God so kind, so good, so overflowing with compassion, I smote upon my breast to think that I could ever have rebelled against One who loved me so and sought my good.[3]

When we finally stop fighting, much like a child, we want to be held. The safest place we can possibly be is in the arms of the One who was once our Adversary and is now our Advocate. The closer we get to Him, the further our fears flee. Additionally, the more our will molds to His will and the more our mind begins to think His thoughts, the more our heart desires His desires.

Allowing God to overpower us means we stop fighting and eliminate all other facades of pleasure or protection. When we understand that following Christ is the best option, we realize we have no reason to fight, no reason to run, no reason to be angry.

WHERE ELSE WOULD I GO?

Jesus, being God Himself, carried this intense and powerful attribute of *El Shaddai*, and He gently overthrew the will of the disciples at times. After a demanding call of discipleship, John tells us, "[M]any of his disciples turned back and no longer walked with him…" (John 6:66). This had to be incredibly disheartening for those who remained with Jesus. They saw the faces of the people they grew up with, perhaps even some of their relatives, walking away from Christ. Feelings of doubt, embarrassment, fear, and anger had to be pumping through their veins.

In the silence of that sobering moment, Jesus asked the remaining disciples a probing question: "Do you want to go away as well?" (v. 67).

Peter answered: "Lord, to whom shall we go? You have the words of eternal life, and we have believed, and have come to know, that you are the Holy One of God" (v. 68–69).

Peter expressed his understanding of their total abandonment by acknowledging what they must not have understood—the fact that Jesus is the Christ, the Son of God who is the Way to eternal life. Peter took a step that many in his day did not or could not take. Peter made the Spirit-guided connection between the words of Jesus and the nature of Jesus Himself.

When Peter placed his faith in the character and words of Jesus, he displayed two great characteristics of his faith. These two beliefs allowed Peter to make an absolute commitment to the Lord Jesus Christ. He said:

"We believe." Peter had *faith*. He had an inward conviction that Jesus was who He claimed to be and accepted His Lordship in his life.

"We know." He *experienced* Christ. Peter and the others had knowledge that came through experiencing changed lives. A changed life, a full heart, and a new desire and direction in life are all too powerful to ignore. Once you truly experience God, there is no denying His impact.

Peter knew how his life was transformed and stated with confidence that he would not walk away. Of course, there came a time of weakness in Peter's life when he failed the Lord. He did turn his back on Jesus for a time, but he did not walk away forever. One of the best definitions for what it means to be a Christian is "the one who cannot walk away."

Once you feel the powerful touch of Almighty God, once you walk in the light of His glory, once you taste of His goodness and experience His best, you will never be satisfied with substitutes and imitations.

WHEN WE ARE DISILLUSIONED, WE FACE A DECISION

Like the fickle followers of Christ who left and walked away, sometimes I hear the Lord whispering, "Do you want to go as well?" If I am honest, at times the answer is yes, I do. Sadly, my heart is prone to wander. It has a predisposition toward selfishness. I consider walking away because I perceive there is an easier route, or at least a more pleasurable one.

The call to follow Christ is hard, even brutal at times. It demands more than I ever have to give. When I realize I have nowhere else to go, I realize I am in desperate need of Jesus. Every other option will leave me shorthanded. Every other option will cause me to find the end of myself and the beginning of... *nothing*. However, when I find the end of myself with Jesus, I find the beginning of *everything* I will ever need.

Everything else that I thought could give me life just drained me of it. Jesus offers me life.

Everything else that I thought would give me hope just stole it. Jesus offers me hope.

Everything else that I thought would give me security made me feel more insecure. Jesus promised to never let me go.

All other options compared to Christ become irrelevant once I truly consider what He is offering. Nothing offers me this kind of life—eternal life that changes this temporary life. Christ is not one option among many; Christ is the option that eliminates all others.

El Shaddai will eventually overpower us all. Even those who do not trust Christ as their Lord will one day all bow the knee and see Him as God when He is fully revealed (Romans 14:11). If we allow Him to overpower us now by faith, He can turn our anxiety into peace, our grieving into comfort, our doubt into belief. He can overpower us, and eventually He will overwhelm us. You can choose to wait. You can continue to carry the weight of your own emotions with unbelieving anger intact.

Or...you can allow Him to win you over today, trusting Him completely with every emotion in your life. As you face your times of anxiety, will you hold on to your anger, or will you trust the overpowering love and sovereignty of God to hold you?

THREE STEPS TOWARD THE END OF ANXIETY

ACT

Make a list of what you "believe" and what you "know" about God. Post these on social media and pray them to God, affirming that what you cling to about His character is the very thing that gives Him the right to "overthrow" your situation and emotions.

REFLECT

Where are you dealing with anger or disappointment with God the most? Honestly confess your resentment toward Him and prayerfully ask Him to help you change your attitude and perspective.

READ

Study Isaiah 40 and see how God comforts His people and encourages us to trust Him.

CHAPTER 4

BECOME BRUTALLY HONEST WITH A GRACIOUS GOD

START WITH SCRIPTURE
Psalm 73

CORE PRINCIPLE FOUR

God created my emotions, and He invites me to process my feelings before Him so He can interact with me, calm me, and change me.

"*If God knows everything, then why should I tell Him anything?*"

Mashala's eyes were dilated, and her hands were fidgeting. It was clear something was bothering her deep inside.

I had just finished speaking to the youth group about how we need to be honest—specifically with God. We spent most of our time talking through six different emotions that often roadblock our honesty: shame, anger, depression, fear, denial, and pride. I placed each of these emotions on large flip boards behind me.

As I greeted Mashala near the stage, her words cut through my heart: "I am all of these, but specifically depressed and angry.

While I heard what you said about being honest with God, I'm not sure I have anything else to tell Him. If God knows everything, then why should I tell Him anything? Doesn't He already know where I'm at?"

I could tell her pain and emotions were deep and excruciating. What she was really asking—and what you may be asking as well—is this: "What's the point of involving God when I am not seeing anything change?"

There is a difference between informing God and drawing close to God. I can inform my friend of something, or I can choose to talk deeply about a topic, grow our friendship, and risk being vulnerable for the sake of greater closeness in our relationship. This is true with God; we can choose to use our prayer life to only inform Him, or we can use it to transform our faith by drawing closer to Him.

Prayer is not telling God something He doesn't already know. Prayer is telling God what He does know and acknowledging that He can do something about it.

Most of us wouldn't dare speak to God the way Job did.

Job asked if it was good for God to watch him flail in misery (Job 10:3). He wasn't focusing on whether or not God's behavior was right. He was focused on the emotional benefit God seemed to gain by watching Job flail around in his life like a bug dying in the dirt.

Job was determined to find out what possible good or pleasure God found by watching him suffer in agony and anxiety.

Job questioned God, but he never seemed to lose sight that God still had the final say. Job's questions weren't meant to challenge God's authority; he simply wanted to know why God wasn't doing something—*anything*—to save him.

When we go through severe pain and punishment from God, it's easy to turn away from Him instead of *toward* Him. Like a child upset with his parents, we turn to beating the chest of our Father rather than finding peace in His loving arms.

Is it wrong to tell God how we feel? Are we sinning when we question His motives and actions?

Honesty with God is only sinful when we move from a place of pursuing answers to pridefully inserting conclusions. Who are we to write the end of the story better than the Author of Life Himself?

You don't know God's mind. I don't know God's mind. Why? Because we are not Him.

Think about needing to go to urgent care or the emergency room. When you arrive, the medical team starts gathering your vital signs. Before they even get to the problem at hand, they want to take your blood pressure and listen to your heart and lungs. After the vitals are collected, they then focus on the problem you're experiencing right now:

When did it start?

Where does it hurt?

What makes it worse?

These data-gathering questions are used to identify what exactly is going on in your physical body so they can help heal you. They don't just poke, prod, and puncture without good information about where to start working.

When it comes to our emotions, we are invited to share with God the vitals and facts about our pain. We start with the emotional health of our hearts and lungs; metaphorically, how we feel about what we're experiencing and how it's bringing or taking life from our souls. This is why the Psalmist's words echo with ours: "My heart is melting, my breath has left me, etc." And then we are honest and even factual about the turmoil we're experiencing. We tell God, "This is when it started... This is where it hurts the most... This is what makes it worse..."

Mashala's words may stick in your mind as they still do in mine: "But why tell God if He already knows?" It is not that God doesn't know. Of course He already knows, since He knows everything—but by telling Him honestly about your pain, it invites God to begin a greater work in you.

In one of my earlier books, *Honest to God: Becoming Brutally Honest with a Gracious God*, I set out to prove the hypothesis in my life and in others' that honesty is not an end in and of itself, but it is a means to our transformation.

We are not sharing things with God, the Great Physician, for the sake of simply saying something and getting it off our chests. We are being honest with God because this tells the Great Physician that we're ready and willing for Him to begin His work of healing our hearts.

Now I want to be careful here. While I know that not all anxiety comes from unconfessed sin in our lives, that *can* be one cause of anxiety. God can allow angst and discomfort in our lives because of sin that we've hidden and left unconfessed. Perhaps the best biblical analogy that God gave us for this comes from an Old Testament story.

When God told the nation of Israel to destroy remnants of its victory at Jericho, a man named Achan stole from what God told them to destroy and hid the plunder under his tent. Even though Achan thought he buried the spoils well, God knew about it, and God's anger burned against all the people of Israel because of Achan's sin (Joshua 7:1). The Israelites even lost a battle over it, and thirty-six men died because God removed His protections due to Achan's unconfessed sin.

God withheld His sovereign blessing until the nation of Israel dealt with the sin. He told Joshua, "I will not be with you anymore unless you destroy whatever among you is devoted to destruction" (Joshua 7:12). God called out the hidden sin to Joshua; Joshua called out the sin among all the people of Israel, including Achan. When the truth came out, the angst was over. Achan (and his family) lost their lives over the matter, but Joshua 7 ends by saying, "The Lord was no longer angry."

I am pretty sure I've had an "Achan" season in my own life. There has been at least one punctuated season I can point to where I thought my sin, though it was stopped and confessed to a few trusted believers, was still buried under my tent. It wasn't until I came clean with the Lord and others whom I had hurt that I felt God's anger with me subside. Looking back, I regret ever doing it, and even more so, I regret that it took me so long to fully confess my sin.

Confessing our sins is essential to salvation. If we confess our sins and have faith, then we will be saved by the blood of Jesus. However, this is not just something we do to be saved; it is what we do continually *when we are saved.*

Reading 1 John 1:9 in context, we understand that we need ongoing confession to remain in fellowship with God and with others.

The act of confession applies to both our fellowship with God and with man. It is continually "owning our messes" by telling God and others how we have sinned against Him and others.

This idea of confessing our sins to each other is not a major theme in the New Testament. There are only a few cases of public confession of sin in the New Testament:

- John the Baptist (Matthew 3:6; Mark 1:15)
- When people need healing (James 5:16)
- When they burned magical books (Acts 19:18)

While John may have in mind some public confession or speaking about our sins to other people, it is more about living true to God and not hiding that you are a sinner. It may not mean that you confess specific sins to all people, but only to those you have wronged.

Maybe you've been in a prayer meeting or small group where the idea of confessing your sins comes up. All of a sudden, you start sweating in places you didn't know you could sweat because you are afraid you are going to have to share your sin with the world. I get that. But let's be clear about what the Bible is talking about when it mentions confession.

Sharing my sin with another person doesn't make me forgiven. God is the only One who can forgive (Isaiah 43:25; Daniel 9:9; Mark 2:7). However, when we see confession mentioned in the New Testament, we see the concept aligned with what is written 1 John 1:9. Live in the light, admit that you are a sinner, and pursue forgiveness through the blood of Jesus.

When we are confessing our sins to one another, there is no room for reliving it in the retelling. There should not be anything sensational about the mutual confessing of sin, nothing that feeds sinful desires (Galatians 6:1–2). Rather, we take on a posture like that of King David in Psalm 51; our confession should be the humble acknowledgment of the act of sin and the joy of release from the offensiveness of those acts.

If our offense is against someone specifically, we are to go to them and ask for forgiveness before we worship God. The whole idea of Scripture when it comes to confession is (1) to make right where we've gone wrong and (2) never hide the fact that we need Jesus.

Our mutual confession must lead to mutual prayer. Although believers bear one another's burdens, nothing in confession should spawn temptation and sinful acts.

As it relates to confession with God, we bear the full responsibility of confession. We never have to fear that if we say what we did God will hold it against us. Rather, He is faithful and just to forgive us for the sins we committed.

Our confession to God invites His forgiveness to invade our lives. When we stop trying to hide from God, He purifies and cleanses us from our sins. Max Lucado writes,

> Confession does for the soul what preparing the land does for the field. Before the farmer sows the seed, he works the acreage, removing the rocks and pulling the stumps. He knows that seed grows better if the land is prepared. Confession is the act of inviting God to walk the acreage of our hearts. "There is a rock of greed over here, Father; I can't budge it. And that tree of guilt near the fence? Its roots are too long and deep. And may I show you some dry soil too crusty for seed?" God's seed grows better in the soil of the heart if cleared.[1]

The passage says He is "faithful and just to forgive us our sins and cleanse us of all unrighteousness." The idea that God is "faithful and just" hearkens back to Exodus 34:6–7:

> The LORD passed before him and proclaimed, "The LORD, the LORD, a God merciful and gracious, slow to anger, and abounding in steadfast love and faithfulness, keeping steadfast love for thousands, forgiving iniquity and transgression and sin."

God will forgive us just as He said He would if we only take the time to confess how our hearts have wronged Him. God is not just faithful; He is just. This most certainly means that He is righteous: acting in accordance with His character, never slipping in His standards or His promised Word.

Knowing that God gave His Word, the passage concludes by saying, "Don't make Him out to be a liar" because God never lies.

If we say we have not sinned, we make Him a liar, and His Word is not in us (1 John 1:10).

John didn't choose to sugarcoat the severe truth of confession. He didn't just say, "You make God sad when you accept your sin as normal and cover up your brokenness." He went further by saying, "You make God out to be a liar."

Mashala's question wasn't about being depressed or angry; it was about honesty. As we've seen with each previous chapter, anxiety ignites a question of God's sovereignty. For all of the midnight and midday moments of terror, for the moments where you and I feel trapped in the suffocating grip of anxiety, where's God? Why isn't He doing something—*anything*—to get me out of this?

If we want to see the end of anxiety, it starts with honesty. I can't pretend that shaking free of anxiety is within my power. It's not, but it's within His power.

What is within my power is confessing any sin that may be standing in the way of peace.

What is within my power is admitting I am *not* God, and He is the one with a sovereign plan.

What is within my power is walking the journey, even in the darkest moments of life, by following His pathway through Scripture, prayer, worship, and silence until His voice speaks into my heart.

The purpose of anxiety is to remind our hearts of the goodness, grace, and sovereignty of our Savior. The One who breathed planets into orbit is the only One who allows the whirlwind of anxiety to stir our hearts toward Him. When we acknowledge that stirring of our souls is when we can see what Jesus is going to do next in the storm.

THREE STEPS TOWARD THE END OF ANXIETY

ACT

Is there someone you need to go confess your sin to, owning where you went off course and caused them pain? Take time to make that call, meet with them, or write that letter acknowledging your own wrongdoing and asking for their forgiveness.

MEMORIZE

Commit 1 John 1:9–10 to memory.

REPENT

Repentance is when the Holy Spirit enables a supernatural change of our motive, thoughts, and behavior. What areas need to change in your life? Ask God to help you recognize and repent.

HOW CAN I GAIN CONTROL WHEN I FEEL OUT OF CONTROL?

CHAPTER 5

ENDURING DOUBT

START WITH SCRIPTURE
Hebrews 12:1–11

CORE PRINCIPLE FIVE

Life is a marathon, not a sprint, and the sin of doubting God's sovereignty can weigh us down. It's our sacred responsibility to be honest about where our doubts and anxiety may lead us and build our foundation on our Savior and His Word.

It had to be well over 110 degrees, but it felt even hotter. No man has ever walked on the surface of the sun, but if anyone has come close to experiencing what that would feel like, we did. We were hiking in the desert of Israel on the hottest day ever recorded for October. I asked the bus driver to pull over and let us off. He seemed confused because there was nothing on the road but a guardrail and a bunch of trash.

The fifty people I was leading thought I was crazy to get them off the air-conditioned bus and encourage them to hop over the guardrail and start hiking, but I wanted to show them something.

We started walking across the white stone and dirt intermingled with the occasional broken bottle and empty wrapper. We soon came upon a valley that looked like a dry riverbed. Instead of walking around this twenty- to thirty-foot-wide ravine, I led our group into it, and we started hiking along, longing for any shade from the surrounding valley walls. It was almost noon, and there was no escaping the blistering sun.

I was carrying my one-year-old son, who weighed twenty-seven pounds, in a hiking backpack. I stopped a time or two to have surrounding hikers check him and ensure he was doing OK, since it felt like he was overheating on my back. Finally, we came upon a shrub—maybe more like an overgrown weed, but it was something big enough for a few people to find a bit of shade. We gathered as close to that prickly bush as we could in hopes of finding some covering, and I removed my son from my backpack.

I am sure some of the hikers were having private conversations with me in their heads for bringing them to such a place. Others were saying out loud, "Whatever you're trying to show us, it better be worth it!"

I took them into the desert and down into this valley to show them what the Bible, and Jesus specifically, meant when He called us to be steadfast.

"I brought you into this valley," I announced at the top of my lungs, "to show you this valley."

Spoiler alert: they were not amused.

"Seriously?! We could have seen this from the bus," someone retorted.

"Yes, while you could have seen it from the bus, you couldn't have *experienced* it from the bus," I said. "This valley is one of the most dangerous places to be in all of Israel, not because of the heat but because of water."

The ravine where we were standing is called a *wadi*. Throughout the desert south of Jerusalem and other parts of Israel, the ground at the bottom of a *wadi* is dusty, gritty, and lined with gravel from years of rainstorms driving water deep into the dirt and carving out these ravines.

On the sides of the ravines are massive walls of stone formed over hundreds of years. In some cases, these stone walls are even granite, and there are caves in different areas along the *wadi* hedges. The walls are beautiful to look at, and I marvel at their strength.

The danger comes when a small amount of rain pours down around Jerusalem, to the north of where we stood. The desert ground can't absorb the rainwater fast enough, and in a matter of minutes, it can create flash floods that surge through the *wadis*.

The leading cause of death among tourists in Israel isn't heat-related; it's drowning from flash floods. I had to make sure it hadn't rained up north near Jerusalem beforehand because it would have been life-threatening for us to be down in the *wadi*.

In our brief time there, we looked at Matthew 7, the Sermon on the Mount, where Jesus talks about building your house on the rock:

> Everyone then who hears these words of mine and does them will be like a wise man who built his house on the rock. And the rain fell, and the floods came, and the winds blew and beat on that house, but it did not fall, because it had been founded on the rock. And everyone who hears these words of mine and does not do them will be like a foolish man who built his house on the sand. And the rain fell, and the floods came, and the winds blew and beat against that house, and it fell, and great was the fall of it (Matthew 7:24–27).

Jesus wasn't saying, "Don't build your house on a sandy beach." If you've never seen a *wadi*, it's easy for us to imagine Jesus was talking about building your house on the shores of San Diego. That was not the kind of sand Jesus had in mind. Instead, He was saying, "Don't build your house on the sandy bottom of the *wadi*." The only wise place to be when the flash floods come is to be standing on the firm, granite-like rock on the side of the ravine.

Jesus's words drive us to consider our foundation. We need to build every area of our lives on the foundation of God's Word and the Rock of our salvation, Jesus Christ. It's not a matter of *if* but *when* the storms of life come crashing our way. The waters *will* rise. The floods *will* come. When the sudden surging rivers of anxiety and fear come crashing into our lives, is our foundation built to withstand the flood?

The writer of Hebrews gives us an amazing call to steadfastness and endurance in Hebrews 12:1–11. This passage starts with the two verses that you have heard quoted before:

> Therefore, since we are surrounded by such a great cloud of witnesses, let us throw off everything that hinders and the sin that so easily entangles. And let us run with perseverance the race marked out for us, fixing our eyes on Jesus, the pioneer and perfecter of faith. For the joy set before Him, He endured the cross, scorning its shame, and sat down at the right hand of the throne of God (Hebrews 12:1–2 NIV).

THE SIN THAT SO EASILY ENTANGLES

Sin is sticky and heavy, like a dark, staining tar invading our souls and clogging our hearts. The writer of Hebrews may have had all sin in mind, but in this situation, "sin" is likely referring to the root of all sin, and perhaps the most elusive and invasive sin: doubting God.

I live in Colorado, where we have some of the most avid running communities in the world. Marathon runners, Spartan race runners, endurance runners, triathletes—these are my neighbors, friends, and people in our church. Many don't realize that being a runner has as much to do with your mental strength and endurance as it does with your physical running ability. That's why runners try to eliminate any unnecessary weight before they run. Serious runners are fitted for appropriately sized shoes and gear, even choosing specific socks to wear to give their feet the optimal comfort without causing friction that can affect their endurance and movement. They train for optimal body composition by not packing on a lot of extra muscle and by focusing on a set regimen of exercises.

Anything that might hinder a runner's endurance can make all the difference between an amazing run or failing to reach the finish line. In the same way, we can't expect to complete the race of life with the weight of doubt burdening our hearts and minds.

If we are going to run with endurance, not only does our foundation need to be solid, but our sprinting needs to be unhindered. Meaning: we need to shed the unnecessary doubt that easily clings to us and cling to truth instead.

Having questions and uncertainty is not sin. It's the doubt of God's sovereignty, a shadow of skepticism that can cloud your faith—and allowing it to linger—that leads to sin. It's the question of "I don't think God's really in control, so what's the point?" or "God's not showing up how I want Him to show up, and I doubt He'll ever show up. It's up to me to take matters into my own hands. I need to do God's job for Him…"

That doubt, and the attempt to supersede God's sovereignty, is what drove Abram (later Abraham) and Sarai (later Sarah) to enlist Hagar, Sarai's Egyptian servant, to conceive with Abram. They doubted God's timing (Genesis 16:1). We cannot expect to run the race of life unless we trust the sovereignty of God in *every* area of our lives, especially in our darkest moments of uncertainty.

As followers of Jesus, we need to look at verse 1 again and wonder, "How does the sin that so easily entangles show up in my life?" Certainly, you have questioned God's sovereign and powerful control before—we all have. What you do with this questioning is what matters most.

Doubt is the skeleton that faith grows on. If I take the doubts I have to God and ask Him to work with me on them, I find that He can bring the fresh air of faith to me in such a profound way. Only one thing can happen when I take my doubt to God: my trust in Him will grow. My questions don't matter as much because I know the One who holds the answers. That is when we truly toss aside the weight of doubt and run freely toward our good Heavenly Father.

GET OVER THE WALL

While having the right body composition, diet, and running gear is important for running a great race physically, the mental endurance needed for long-distance running is just as important. Runners talk about hitting "the wall"—around mile twenty—when all glycogen (energy stores) is depleted. You start to feel lightheaded, even nauseous; your eyes start blurring a bit, and you feel weak.

That's the moment when the little voice in the back of your mind starts whispering:

You don't have what it takes.

This is too hard—you're never gonna make it.

You'll never finish this race.

You should just quit now and face the shame of not finishing ...

Hitting "the wall" is where most marathon runners quit—even though many, if not most, have the physical capability of running the full race. Those who quit haven't prepared their minds for the mental endurance the race will demand.

What about those who push past the wall? What's their secret? The crowd. It is those lining the race who are cheering, pushing, and shouting encouragement: "You can do it! You're almost there! This part is the worst, but you can make it!"

As followers of Jesus, we each have our race to run in life, and we're surrounded by those who've gone before us who know the pain and agony of pushing through the grueling grind of whatever life throws their way. These are the ones whose lives inspire us to follow their example, whether they're with us still or reside now in Heaven.

I think of Maureen, my wife's mom, now in Heaven, as one who pushed through worry and fear in her life to receive the prize of Christ. I think of my best friend, Keith, who was taken at the age of forty-two by cancer but sprinted through chemo, radiation, and endless nights of suffering, panic, and anxiety to finally fall into the arms of Christ. What about Abraham, Moses, Job, David, Esther, Isaiah, the disciples, or Paul? These great heroes of the faith had their moments of doubt, but they pressed beyond the wall to find victory in Christ on the other side.

Ultimately, we're encouraged to look at the example of Christ and His resurrection as the reward for pushing through doubts to run the race marked out for us. Christ and His Word are the supreme inspirations for our faith. He is the reason for our repentance. He is the One we cling to in the moments of anxiety and doubt. He is the One we can trust with our past, present, and future.

Verses 3–11 of Hebrews 12 remind us that this race we call life demands endurance. Throughout this chapter, we encounter the word "endurance." Its basic meaning in the original translation is "to remain in place, to stand firm." We see a nuance of this term in two places in Matthew: "You will be hated by everyone because of me, but the one who stands firm to the end will be saved" (Matthew 10:22); and "but the one who stands firm to the end will be saved" (Matthew 24:13).

Luke uses the same word to describe one of the seeds in the Parable of the Sower: "The seed on good soil stands for those with a noble and good heart, who hear the Word, retain it, and by persevering produce a crop" (Luke 8:15). Famously, Paul writes in his letter to the Romans: "We also glory in our sufferings, because we know that suffering produces perseverance; perseverance, character; and character, hope" (Romans 5:3–4).

In these examples, there is an element of waiting, of holding out until a designated time or until the end. In verse 3, the writer of Hebrews implores the reader to consider Jesus as one who endured opposition. The reader is encouraged to think about this for a purpose: so that you—the one who will face opposition, uncertainty, and even doubt—will endure and not lose heart.

Jesus looked beyond the shame and suffering of the cross to see the joy set before Him. He got over the wall for joy on the other side.

There are so many fears threatening to hold us back, as we see in verse 1. These fears are our pasts, our broken identities, beliefs, and choices we hold on to that are defining a bankrupt version of our souls. Repentance isn't just turning away from the act of sinning; it's getting away from the doubting and trap of thinking that God is not enough. Repentance is turning away from self-sufficiency and declaring God-dependency.

What's causing anxiety in your life currently? Now is your chance to turn away from your mistakes, wounds, self-inflicted damage, or the sin of doubt that may be weighing you down. Now is your chance to let go of someone else's idea of who you should be or what you should do. Build a strong foundation by leaning into the truths of Scripture and reminding yourself of the profound freedom found in the Gospel. That is the foundation that can withstand any flood of anxiety, doubt, fear, or panic.

IT DOESN'T MAKE SENSE!

As I was driving to my writing spot today, I made a phone call to a woman in our church who just lost her forty-nine-year-old son. He wasn't feeling well, went to the bathroom, and collapsed on the floor, never to live again. His mother cannot get her mind around why God allowed this loss. I can't get my mind around it either. It has been six months now since his passing, and her anger and anxiety continue to grow.

My very human, prayer-driven voicemail to her today went something like this:

"Edie, I cannot imagine how upset you are over the loss of your son. Your husband told me that the waves of grief are pounding against your life right now worse than before. I know my recent message about praying to God in desperation only had to hurt worse because you have prayed desperately, and God is not providing clarity. But while we may never get our questions answered, we know who is holding the answers and who is holding the person asking the questions. May He keep holding you still, Edie. He is still in control even when it doesn't feel that way."

God's ways are not our ways (Isaiah 55:8), which is a near-guarantee that we will experience doubt and skepticism. Our limited human knowledge cannot possibly fathom the depth of God's omniscient ways. If we knew everything He knew, we would pray differently and trust Him more, and it would frighten our hearts with immense dread knowing the full weight God carries on behalf of the world's anxiety. To tackle the anxiety that overwhelms us means we need to rely on the God who overthrows us. Instead of shaking our fists at God, we scream at the waves of doubt with the white-knuckled, vomit-suppressing, pulse-raising faith of "Bring it on, I am not moving!" That is endurance. That is faith that braces for impact well before the flood ever arrives.

GET TO HIGHER GROUND

After we finished talking about Matthew 7 at the bottom of the *wadi*, I encouraged our group to follow me back to our tour bus before the floodwaters came. They were never more relieved to hike out of the canyon, to escape the heat of the desert, and find relief in air conditioning.

Looking back at the opening of that *wadi*, I am reminded how quickly anxiety can flood our hearts, especially when it's least expected. The foundation we build now on the solid rock of our salvation is what will help us endure whatever comes our way.

THREE STEPS TOWARD THE END OF ANXIETY

REFLECT

Read Romans 5:3–4 again, and for each mention of the words "perseverance," "character," or "hope," write down at least three corresponding ways you see God developing you in these areas.

DISCUSS

Meet with a friend and discuss what sin of doubt may "so easily entangle" you and what you could do to stand strong the next time you face those doubts.

READ

Get a copy of Elyse Fitzpatrick's devotional *Doubt: Trusting God's Promises*. Start this thirty-one-day journey to learn how to battle doubts.

CHAPTER 6

FINDING JOY AND PEACE IN THE PAIN

START WITH SCRIPTURE
Philippians 4:4–7

CORE PRINCIPLE SIX

When it comes to finding peace, we often look to counterfeit comforts. We look for things that will bring us momentary pleasure or ease our pain. The power of God offers joy and peace, no matter our emotions or circumstances.

The people of Philippi never forgot what happened when Paul was in prison in their town. We read the riveting story in Acts 16. It was about midnight as Paul and Silas were singing hymns and praying from their chained-up position in the guarded jail cell. Suddenly, what felt like an earthquake shook the wall and set the men free! The guard was so distraught over his perceived failure of losing the prisoners that he attempted to commit suicide. Right before piercing his own heart, he was interrupted by Paul and Silas. They assured him all the prisoners were still inside. Paul and Silas could have run free, but instead they used that moment to lead the prison guard to faith in Christ, which later led to his whole family believing as well.

Fast-forward ten years: Paul is in prison again in Rome, writing to the Church of Philippi from a different jail cell. Paul knows about the anxiety and doubt many in the Philippian Church are experiencing. He hopes to comfort them by reminding them that joy and peace are found in the midst of pain. Sometimes the work of God in our lives is easily forgotten because of the flood of emotions we feel.

The Philippians knew what God did in their past, but they struggled to trust Him with their anxieties in the present. Sound familiar? I know I've been there as well.

The Philippians' distraught feelings are not much different than ours at times. Sure, we have technology, religious freedom, longer lifespans, and liberties they didn't have, but we share the human side of having feeble faith. The Philippians of the first century experienced anxiety just like us:

- Anxiety about provision because they needed money and a place to meet together as a church
- Anxiety about cultural unrest
- Anxiety about being marginalized as followers of Jesus
- Anxiety about doctrinal issues from people who opposed the Gospel because of selfish ambition or some form of legalism
- Anxiety about disagreements or tensions within the church

Even though they saw the power of God in the past and they knew the joy of Christ, they still experienced moments of spiritual amnesia. They forgot what God can do and how He can show up in even the worst moments in life.

At times, our anxiety and depression can feel more real to us than the power of God. He desires that we experience joy and peace by His power, no matter our feelings. Let's enter the Philippians' story by reading what Paul penned in Philippians 4:4–7:

> Rejoice in the Lord always; again I will say, rejoice. Let your reasonableness be known to everyone. The Lord is at hand; do not be anxious about anything, but in everything by prayer and supplication with thanksgiving let your requests be made known to God. And the peace of God, which surpasses all understanding, will guard your hearts and your minds in Christ Jesus.

Paul starts with a command, not a soft suggestion: "Rejoice in the Lord always!" This command of "rejoice" is to renew or return joy to our lives. No matter the situation in which we find ourselves, we must always rejoice.

Joy is not tied to circumstances. Paul is encouraging his readers, including us today, to have joy—not just sometimes or when things are going well. Joy and peace are perspectives, not coping mechanisms.

The peace of God that is available to us is not merely the absence of disappointment, sorrow, hurt, or hardship. Paul is instructing his original readers—and us—to change our outlook on any circumstance.

It is often those who seem to have easy lives who find it most difficult to maintain true joy and peace because they are bombarded almost daily with a host of counterfeits. Counterfeit joy disguises itself as "happiness" in how we feel pleasure over possessions, physical fitness, sufficient income, or sexual fulfillment.

There is also a counterfeit peace prancing around our lives as "harmony" in the form of popularity, notoriety, and prosperity.

While these things may be good and may even be gifts from the Lord, they are conditional, temporary, and dependent on you or someone else doing what you want them to do.

If joy and peace are going to pass the test of time, they must be based on something far greater than the fickleness of humanity and the frailty of circumstances. Paul made the audacious command that we are to rejoice always—in spite of others or circumstances—because he is basing these perspectives on the immutability of God.

Paul's reasons for asserting that we should have joy and peace are two-fold:

The first is because we are "in the Lord." Having joy outside the Lord is a counterfeit joy—it is superfluous, superficial, and temporary. "Rejoice in the Lord" is realizing you are made new in Him. No matter any loss or gain in this life, if you have Jesus, He is all you need.

The truly godly person longs for God's presence, where we point our hearts to God in joy with prayer and thanksgiving and live with a constant acknowledgment that our lives belong to God. We realize and rejoice in the fact that Jesus is alive and brings us life.

The second assertion Paul makes is this: "The Lord is close at hand." There are two implications to this statement: one is related to time and the other to space.

Time: "The Lord is at hand" can be read as a reminder of the nearness of His coming; this is Paul's way of reminding his readers that Jesus is returning, and possibly soon. Therefore, they are to act accordingly and admit their anxiety to God so He can sustain their hearts until they are fully in His presence.

Space: "The Lord is at hand" can also relate to closeness in proximity; it is Paul's way of reminding us of Jesus's nearness here and now through the Spirit. Jesus is "nearer than our breath," as the Psalmist says (Psalm 46:10). The Lord is already close to us; He is not a far-off God.

With these two truths in mind, the reason we can have joy and peace is because of the reality of His future reign and the closeness of Christ.

The ideas of "joy" and "peace" are not escapism; they are not ways of pretending things are fine when they are not, but they are fixed on reality. The joy and peace Christ offers are ways of seeing current events in light of eternity and anticipating the lasting comfort that will come at Christ's second coming. The chief end of anxiety is to help us move toward God and gain an overwhelming sense of peace that Jesus is already with us and is coming again.

We are anxious people because we are broken people. We all live in a fallen world, and the real miracle is that we are not all in a continual panic attack. Christians are not immune to the circumstances of this world that bring anxiety and depression. These feelings are very human experiences. Romans 8:22–23 says we live in a world groaning and waiting for redemption. The default language of all humans is groaning and grumbling. It's no wonder that overwhelming emotions plague so many of us.

God not only meets us in our struggles; He is sovereign over our struggles. It is not a good feeling to be anxious or depressed, but God will use it. His toolbox is bigger than we think it is; He will do more than we understand in our struggles. It is the power of God through the Holy Spirit that makes the peace and joy of Christ tangible.

IS THAT A PROMISE?

Joy and peace are consistent themes in Paul's letters. In 1 Thessalonians 5:13 and 16, as well as 1 Corinthians 13:11, both joy and peace are commanded, but in the case in Philippians 4:4–7, joy is commanded while peace is promised.

Philippians 4:7 says, "And the peace of God, which surpasses all understanding, will guard your hearts and your minds in Christ

Jesus." It is a promise! The peace He gives will often not make sense to our minds amid our circumstances, but He gives it to us to help guard our hearts and minds in Christ. God is never without power or resources to intervene, yet He asks us to trust that He is in control even before He changes the circumstances. The joy and peace Paul talks about cannot be separated in this promise; to have one is to have both at every point and in every circumstance.

Paul introduces a series of terms and ideas in this passage, the first of which is reasonableness. "Reasonableness" can also be translated as "kindness" or "gentleness." We are to show love, gentleness, and kindness toward others. Paul includes this as an antidote to anxiety and depression: be kind to others.

That seems like an odd place to call people to be kind. I know when I am anxious or depressed, the last thing I want to do is care about someone else. My Cheetos and couch are far more inviting than selflessly serving someone else, but that is Paul's point!

Practicing joy is far more than an "inner peace" I bring myself through self-help or self-loathing. Practicing joy should be in our relationships with others. It is why Paul brings up gentleness. Genuine Christian joy is not found by looking inward. Joy is found upward and outward; it is through concentrating on God's ability to help me fulfill the needs of others that we learn to rejoice—even in suffering.

In arguably my worst season of anxiety, I forced myself to sit in my big brown pleather (plastic-leather) chair in the mornings and read the prayer requests of our church. The last thing I wanted to do was hear about anyone else's problems. But by forcing myself to read and pray for those who were also suffering, I found a sense of joy and peace. It was not because their problems were worse than mine—many of them were not. But by interceding for others, I was running to the throne of grace and remembering that God was my refuge in times of trouble (Psalm 9:9–10)—any trouble.

The second action of joy and peace Paul gives is perhaps the one we need the most: "do not be anxious about anything." Often, we use Christian language to drum up false motivation in the name of positivity, as if the goal were to get a person to minimize their pain or problem and think "happy Jesus thoughts." **I cannot emphasize enough how dangerous it is to tell someone you know with anxiety to "get over it."** Skeptics are right to point out how thoroughly unhelpful and unloving that approach is. The Gospel teaches that God's glory is found in weakness, whether it's anxiety, worry, or depression. Never are we called to ignore a problem of pain and act like it doesn't exist. We do not need to minimize or whitewash what is happening. We must find Christ in the midst of what is happening and embody His compassion.

Christ offers us a better alternative to the chaotic and contradictory ideas of being happy and accepting shallow Christianity. True biblical joy is rooted in truth—not prose, possessions, or circumstances. We don't have to be anxious about anything because Christ is King, and He is good and loving. He is in control, even when it does not feel that way based on what we can only see right now.

BUT...

After being told to be anxious about nothing, we are instructed to fill that void with prayer. The third action Paul calls us to is prayer and supplication. Prayer is a key, indispensable element in battling and overcoming anxiety—not an afterthought. The idea of supplication is to "plea humbly." It is asking, begging, and trusting that God will hear us and do what is best for His glory and our eternity.

Paul couples the action of prayer with an invitation: "Let your request be known to God." There is no woe-is-me attitude here that is supposed to keep us from asking the Father for what we want or need. Instead, after thanking Him for His goodness and setting

aside our anxiety (at least for a moment), we are invited to let Him
know what we desire or need.

There are times when the weight of the world will not let us
pray with anything more than just a groan. I know that feeling of
being crushed under anxiety, and the only words and thoughts we
can eke out are faint cries for supernatural help. Our prayers,
whether they're only groans or actual words, are our cries for help
to the Lord. Prayer can be difficult, especially in moments of anxiety. Nonetheless, the Bible invites us to pray regularly and tell God
what we need. While He already knows what we need (even better
than we do), He welcomes us to pray and, in doing so, dispel our
anxiety as we increase our trust.

THE ANXIETY BOX

Once when I was preaching about battling anxiety with faith
in Christ, I shared this passage from Philippians 4. We then spent
time praying for our anxieties, worries, and depression right there
in the service. I asked everyone to write on a card whatever was
overwhelming their hearts and minds and pray to God about what
they wrote. After spending moments praying alone and together
for these things, I pulled out a box that I call my "Anxiety Box." I
have Philippians 4:4–6 pasted on the front of the box.

I invited everyone to come forward and place their card in this
box. This action would be our declaration that we were surrendering those written-down fears, anxieties, and worries to the Lord
and humbly asking for His help.

Perhaps my favorite moment of the whole night was when
someone in our gathering got up, ran down the aisle to the box,
and slammed his card inside as if he was slam-dunking the
winning point of a game. Soon, the whole room followed as I

watched with tears in my eyes as so many of our fellow believers placed their anxieties, fears, and worries inside the truth of God's care.

You can do the same. Slam your anxiety down at the feet of Christ, trusting that the peace of God, which surpasses all understanding, will guard your heart. Perhaps it is time for you to put your anxiety in a box—or the trash. Whatever is on your heart, take out a piece of paper or a card and write that anxiety, fear, or worry on your card. Be as detailed and messy as you like. Hold nothing back. When you're done writing, find a safe place, probably outside, and burn your paper to ashes or tear it to pieces.

As you watch your paper disappear, remember that the God who made you is holding that burden for you so you can find joy and peace in your pain. That is the hope we cling to every day in our Savior Jesus Christ.

THREE STEPS TOWARD THE END OF ANXIETY

ACT

Write down your anxiety, fear, or worry on a card and then give it over to God. In the end, destroy the card, knowing that God will stay true to take care of what you entrust to Him.

REFLECT

The reason we can have joy and peace is because of the reality of His future reign and the closeness of Christ. How and where do you sense the closeness of Christ in your life right now?

PRAY

Send a message to a few friends asking how you can pray for them. Spend time taking your eyes and prayers off of yourself by interceding for others.

CHAPTER 7

NEVER FIGHT ALONE

START WITH SCRIPTURE
Galatians 6:5; 2 Corinthians 4:7–18

CORE PRINCIPLE SEVEN

While anxiety is deeply personal, it cannot be fought by ourselves. We must find the help we need through Christ in community, biblical counseling, and the Body of Christ to find inner peace.

Cemeteries make us feel alone more than anywhere else on earth. My mom makes an annual trip to Cañon City, Colorado, to visit her parents' gravesite. With each passing mile marker over the two-hour drive from Denver, she tells me how the tapes of old memories play through her head. My grandma's tender touch. My grandpa's deep singing voice. The rich and the poor times. The memories of healthy hikes in Ireland or sad battles with brain tumors and strokes—all of which play their bittersweet scenes in my mom's vivid memory.

Mom recently said to me, "I've never felt more alone than when I am standing by my parents' tombstones, and the setting sun casts a shadow on me. There I see my silhouette on the ground between their graves, and I am reminded that I am alone."

Being alone is not only a feeling we experience after someone we love passes away. Loneliness is something we can feel even in our marriages, friendships, and a life crowded with relationships. Loneliness is not the absence of people; it is the absence of a meaningful connection with people.

Anxiety will try to convince you that no one else understands you and no one is for you. Like the instigator in a hockey game, it skates in covertly with ill intentions. Eventually, it rips the emotional shirt off your back in front of everyone. You feel alone, abandoned, and like no one else is fighting for you.

The devil loves to use our most panicked emotions to convince us that we are alone.

But what if loneliness is a feeling created by God that has a profound purpose? What if God is doing something in our feelings of solitude that is developing a deeper trust in His sovereignty?

After all, God created Adam in the Garden of Eden—ALONE. He could have created a whole community at once, or even put a small group together—but He started with one.

I don't know how long it was before Eve came along; no one does. But we do know that whatever amount of time passed—minutes, months, or years—God came back and said, "It is not good for man to be alone." So out of His graciousness, God gave Adam companionship with another person.

Now, one could argue, why did Adam need another person? He had all the animals on earth at his disposal, but not one of them was a suitable companion (Genesis 2)—no, not even the Golden Retriever. Not only did he have all the companionship of creation at his fingertips, but Adam was also in an unhindered relationship with the Creator, God Himself. Was Adam really alone?

He was alone in the sense that God designed humans to share life with other humans. While God is all we need for salvation and sustains us every day, He does so by allowing us to share friendship with other individuals. It is not a weakness or faulty design that we need each other. God created humans with a longing for connection and community. God designed a desire in us for harmony with one another so that we may overcome feelings of isolation and insignificance. Loneliness can be the catalyst for companionship. To sit and wallow in what we don't have doesn't do us any good. Using the longing that we have to be with others can catapult us into meaningful friendships and relationships that bring healing and hope and can make real the presence of God in our lives. Lydia Brownback, author of *Finding God in My Loneliness*, wrote, "God created human beings with a capacity for loneliness so that we would yearn for and find our all in Him."[1]

STRONGER TOGETHER

One of the fundamental strategies for fighting anxiety is to rely on others. That's right; this personal battle you are fighting is not meant for you to conquer on your own.

Sure, you can try to be like Tank Man, the unidentified Chinese man who stood in front of a group of tanks leaving Tiananmen Square on June 5, 1989. There he stood in the middle of the street as an envoy of tanks drove right toward him. He never dropped his grocery bags or even flinched. He stood his ground, and the tanks stopped. Pretend that you are the Tank Man and your anxiety is the tanks—I am going to guess that you've tried this tactic of mustering up your courage alone. You've bit your bottom lip, held back tears, and tried to grind on with life. Perhaps like Tank Man, it worked for a while, but proudly protesting against anxiety will only stave off the angst for so long.

When you give your life to Christ, not only do you embark on a relationship with your Savior, but you also become part of a community. The Church is not a *place* you go on Sundays. The Church is a group of *people* who believe in Jesus Christ and are part of God's New Covenant people group. Through Christ, they are now in a relationship with God, which connects them to others who are part of this covenant. God is the One who transforms people, and those people transform the world by representing God to a world that desperately needs Him. The love we share for one another not only keeps us alive spiritually but is also a display of love to the watching world (John 13:35).

The New Testament uses the phrase "one another" fifty-nine times. While our walk with God has an individual component to it, God intended for us to do life together. It is also impossible for a Christian to experience true life in Christ without maintaining a connection to the Church.

I am keenly aware that the Church in America is declining. We are about a decade behind Europe, and this trend must stop. As a pastor, I never lay awake at night fearful that the Church will go out of business. I know that God will keep the Church alive; it is His design for taking the Gospel to the world. However, I do wonder what it will take for those who claim Christ to realize that the Church is not optional or extracurricular. God designed the Church to be a *must-have* in our lives. A log removed from the fire burns out quickly; a log that stays on the fire provides blazing heat for all around it. In the same way, Christians must stay connected to other Christians— the Church. This is God's design for keeping our spiritual passions lit.

FIGHTING ALONE WILL EVENTUALLY KILL YOU

I would love to know what the mid-battle conversation sounded like in Exodus 17. Moses commanded the Israelite warriors to go out and fight against the Amalek tribe. Moses stood on the top of a nearby hill and watched the battle with the staff of the Lord in his hand. His brother, Aaron, and Hur were with him. God blessed Moses's leadership and faith in an odd way that day, but in a way that made clear his need for others.

Whenever Moses held up his hand, Israel prevailed, and whenever he lowered his hand, Amalek prevailed (Exodus 17:11).

Now think about it for a moment: They are up on the hill and somehow figure out (the hard way?) that whenever Moses's arms get tired and fall, the men start losing the battle. Yet when he keeps his arms high, they win.

When the lightbulb came on for Moses that his arms were seemingly tied to the power of God over their enemy, was he worried? Did he get a bit panicked or anxious that his now-weary and shaking arms were starting to fall, and this could cost people their lives? Through his dripping sweat and shaking voice, did he finally yell:

"Hey guys, grab my arms!"

It was a cry of desperation from Moses that caused Aaron and Hur to pull up a rock for Moses to sit on so they could hold up his arms (v. 12). It was an odd weakness that was overcome with the power of the community. Did God need Moses's arms to stay high to win that battle? No, of course not. But by lifting Moses's arms, he learned the power of camaraderie like he had not experienced before. I am going to guess that Moses was insistent about having people with him for the rest of his life whenever he went to do God's work.

THE PROGRESSION OF CHRISTIAN CAMARADERIE

Getting to an Aaron-and-Hur kind of dependency is a process. In this world of rugged individualism, we need the Holy Spirit's power to help us develop an acceptance of asking others for help. Here is how I see Scripture providing a framework for this process:

Acceptance—realizing I am alone and accepting others into my life as Christ has welcomed me (Romans 15:7).

Devotion—committing myself to others with brotherly affection for the sake of spurring one another on to be more like Christ (Romans 12:10).

Support—bearing one another's burdens and remaining faithful even when times get tough (Galatians 6:2).

Unity—resolving to never fight alone until Christ returns (1 John 1:7).

Let's take a few minutes to expound on these deeply and identify why each aspect is important and how we can apply it.

Acceptance

Culture cultivates counterfeit connections for us all the time. My phone just dinged to tell me that someone had looked at my LinkedIn page. My Instagram tells me the number of "likes" I have the moment I open the app. Facebook fills my newsfeed with all the people it believes I care about and to whom I am connected. By just looking at my phone, I can feel a sense of connection. Yet while social media may provide some connection to others, it can also provide a false sense of community. We can *feel* like we have lots of friends, but in reality, we are isolated and alone.

We begin our pathway to greater connection by acknowledging that we *need* connection. God welcomes us into a relationship with Him through Christ, and we are to be like Him and welcome others into our lives. We strive to live in harmony with one another (Romans 12:6; 15:5), no matter the cost. Spending ourselves for others usually comes back with a big payout.

Devotion

Once we see that our Christian life is not meant to be lived on some spiritual island, we move to the mainland of devotion to God and His people. Paul wrote, "Be devoted...in brotherly affection" to others. It means that we will risk letting others into our world, as well as getting into theirs. Vibrant relationships demand vulnerability. Yes, you may get hurt, but the goal of the Christian life is not to get to the end safely with as few relational wounds as possible. The goal is to be more like Christ, getting to the end as He did, laying our lives down for others.

Elisabeth Elliot, a woman who knew grief, loss, and worry well, wrote, "To love means to open ourselves to suffering. Shall we shut our doors to love, then and 'be safe?' That's the only alternative. But locking ourselves up and never facing another person won't fix what's going on in our souls."[2]

We risk opening ourselves up, and then we forgive when we are hurt. Ephesians 4:32 says, "Be kind to one another, tenderhearted, forgiving one another, as God in Christ forgave you." A devoted follower of Christ will also be devoted to other followers of Christ.

Support

As we live out our relationships, there will always be *give and take*. Biblical Christian relationships are never one-sided. We must "bear one another's burdens, and so fulfill the law of Christ" (Galatians 6:2). We must be willing to give and accept support as much as we are able.

While I have given support to some of my closest companions, their support in my times of need has gotten me through some of my darkest moments. For example, one summer evening, I was managing our five kids while my wife was at an event. We stayed home and were hanging out with neighbors, enjoying the summer evening. From the outside, everything was fine. But on the inside, I was an anxious mess. I couldn't eat the Indian food my neighbors had labored over and served us all, and some people even asked, "Why are you not eating?" When

I thought I was masking my anxiety well, a kid would scream or hit another kid, and the chaos nearly sent my already-racing heart into cardiac arrest.

At one point, I walked home, carrying my youngest child in my arms. I left the other kids to play, and I closed the door on the neighborhood just to breathe for a minute. Breathing in air felt more like sucking in peanut butter. I felt like I might pass out or lose my mind any minute. Once I caught my cool, I resolved to head back over to the neighbors' home. But as I opened the door to my house, my phone rang.

It was Adam. He is a faithful friend who rarely calls but almost always texts. God knew I needed to hear the voice of reason—which happened to come through his voice that night. Our call wasn't long, and I even told him that I was shocked that he was calling on a Saturday night. He said, "I know I never call like this, especially on the weekend...but God laid you on my heart, and I had no choice but to pick up the phone."

God uses the support of other Christians who are compelled by His Spirit to make His presence tangible. Adam prayed for me and brought the peace of Christ to my life that night.

Unity

Like shattered pieces of glass put back together to make a bowl, so Christians are broken and placed back together by the bond of the Spirit (Ephesians 4:3). Our unity, no matter how broken we may be, is a beautiful container for the Glory of Christ to be held. As we walk through life together, we display the beauty of alignment under Christ, our head. Our unity allows for Christ to be worshiped and the Cross of Jesus Christ to be a message to a disenfranchised and lonely world. Our unity allows us to experience the beauty of the redeeming love of God that forgives us of our sins.

Community has "unity" as its root—our unity allows us to share life with Christ and others.

If we claim that we experience a shared life with Him and continue to stumble around in the dark, we're obviously lying through our teeth—we're not living what we claim. But if we walk in the light, God Himself being the light, we also experience a shared life with one another, as the sacrificed blood of Jesus, God's Son, purges all our sin (Eugene Peterson, *The Message*, 1 John 1:6–7).

ALONE SO YOU WOULD NEVER HAVE TO BE

The truth is that with Christ, you are never truly alone, no matter what you feel. The only one who ever experienced the depths of loneliness was Jesus Himself. He hung on the cross and asked the Father, *"My God, My God, why have You forsaken Me?"* That was the instance of true loneliness—when God the Father turned His face away from the Son. Their bond had always existed, but for that moment, it was severed.

That day on the cross, Jesus experienced true loneliness so you and I would never have to.

THREE STEPS TOWARD THE END OF ANXIETY

ACT

Is there someone you need to reach out to and support right now? Pick up your phone and call or text someone to let them know you are here for them. The timing of your message may be exactly what they need right now.

REFLECT

Where are you trying to do things on your own and not letting others help you? Who could you choose to trust and let in a little bit more, letting them know what you are facing and how you need their help?

ACT

Find a way to do three acts of selflessness by serving someone else and showing random kindness to another person. Pay attention to how helping someone else affects your emotions. Now be open to letting someone else do the same thing for you.

CHAPTER 8

STOP THE REPEAT TRACKS

START WITH SCRIPTURE
Romans 12:1–2; James 1:2–4, 12

CORE PRINCIPLE EIGHT
God gives me hope and help to renew my mind when my thoughts get off track so that I never have to replay the same tracks again. Trusting God in times of turbulence demands that I cling to what is true. The Bible says, "Whatever is true, noble and right...think on such things" (Philippians 4:8).

If you grew up in the '80s and '90s as I did, you're familiar with the idea of mixtapes.

Mixtapes were a way of creating a compilation of music that could be played in any Walkman, car stereo, or boombox. Mixtapes then were what playlists are to us today, except with about one hundred times the effort. If you liked a girl and wanted to give her some music that expressed your deepest feelings, you might have created a mixtape full of Amy Grant songs, maybe a little Backstreet Boys, and some Alanis Morissette. (Or was that just me?)

A mixtape was a real labor of love. You had to have a dual cassette player that could play the tapes you wanted to record on one side of the player while the blank tape—or reused tape from your last girlfriend—was queued to record on the other side. You had to push play and record at the same time, at just the right time, and stop it dead on when the track was over. This dinosaur version of a playlist took a few hours of work to put the thing together. Now do you see why this was such a token of love?

It was not uncommon in the '80s and '90s to be driving down the road and see the insides of a cassette tape strewn all over. The black, thin, shiny film would catch on the nearby weeds or median for dozens of feet. It was as if that discarded, ruined tape let you know someone's heart was broken. Another cassette full of music— likely a mixtape—was gutted out and left for dead. Those songs were long gone, just like that couple's love.

If you're wondering if I ever drove down the road with the window down unrolling the cassette film with every passing mile marker...you are correct. I did. Destroying a mixtape from a past crush had a sense of finality to it that allowed my healing to begin.

RECORDING OVER THE NEGATIVE TRACKS

If only getting rid of annoying, repetitive thoughts were that easy. If only we could get the anxious thoughts plaguing our minds to go away, then maybe our anxiety would stop rearing its restless head.

My wife has dealt with her struggles of nagging thoughts that bring about anxiety. I've watched her say through tears that she wishes the thoughts she keeps having would stop so she could go on with normal life. Sometimes it feels like someone created an awful mixtape of our worst feelings and thoughts, jammed them into the stereo of our mind, cranked the volume to eleven, and snapped off all the control buttons. You can't turn them down or stop hearing the negative tracks no matter what you do.

The truth is that you can't stop some of these "tracks" on your own. You have to welcome the power of God to record over these tracks with healthy, fulfilling tracks of love, compassion, grace, and beauty. The Bible implores us to "take every thought captive to obey Christ" (2 Corinthians 10:5). We can only do this by the power of Christ dwelling in us. My mind must be renewed for my motives to be rewired and my actions to change. I have to "put on" Christ, Paul writes in Romans 13:14, to stop the desires of my flesh that drive me to sin and emotional suffering.

"Do not be conformed to this world, but be transformed by the renewal of your mind, that by testing you may discern what is the will of God, what is good and acceptable and perfect" (Romans 12:2). Without a doubt, my anxious, worried, fearful thoughts are not "acceptable and perfect"—not by my standards or God's. Renewing my thinking means I must record over the lies—the negative "tracks"—I currently believe with the truth God gives me through His Son, His Word, and His Spirit. When Paul says "Be renewed in the spirit of your minds" (Ephesians 4:23), He is commanding and promising that our tracks can be recorded over with new thinking that changes our lives.

MORE THAN COGNITIVE BEHAVIOR THERAPY

Many trained counselors, or even simply well-meaning people in our culture and some churches, will tell us to "think happy thoughts" and get away from what is bringing us down. This strategy is formally called "Cognitive Behavior Therapy" (CBT). It is a form of psychological treatment that some claim is effective for bringing about change in someone's life who is facing depression, anxiety, and grief, as well as situational sadness and overwhelming circumstances. CBT will challenge a person to stop looking at the past and start focusing on their present. The goal of CBT is to change feelings and behaviors by thinking better about life's situations and circumstances. CBT identifies negative thoughts and attempts to replace them with positive thoughts.

While positive thinking may cause a temporary change in emotion and behavior, it does not provide long-term, lasting results. There are minimal side effects to this method of taking care of our problems—other than the massive drawback of someone experiencing failure time and again. Our hope is to find a way not to keep falling into the same hole but to eventually crawl out of it.

While CBT can look similar to biblical Christianity, let me be clear: CBT is not the same as biblical transformation through the only true change agent—our Savior Jesus Christ—and the power of the Gospel. While the Bible teaches the power of renewing our minds, we do so rooted not in mere positivity, but in biblical truth (Romans 12:1–12; Ephesians 4:22–24; Colossians 3:1–10). The Bible tells us that biblical thinking will impact our feelings and actions (John 13:17; James 1:25; Proverbs 29:18). The goal of our thinking is to please God first. Ephesians 5:10 says, "Try and discern what is pleasing to the Lord." When I change my thinking for Him, His Spirit will give me the power to either change my feelings or my perspective. We must recognize that the power of the mind is greater than we think. It forms what we believe in faith and hold as true.

RECORDING NEW TRACKS FOR OUR MINDS TO PLAY

Paul's encouragement to the Philippians was necessary because they were suffering for their faith. Their suffering caused them to be anxious, but they were refusing to let the lies of the enemy win. That is why Paul said to them, "I hear that you are standing firm in one spirit, with one mind striving side by side in faith for the Gospel, and not frightened in anything by your opponents"

(Philippians 1:27–28). They were staying strong and sticking together, even when every outside force—and some inside forces—applied significant pressure to compromise or quit altogether.

The Roman government likely was pressuring them, and as Christianity rose, so did its unpopularity. The cultural tension would have caused anxiety for a first-century Christian who was trying not to rock the boat on the political landscape while living out an authentic faith. There was fear of Rome overthrowing the Church and a fear of the Church conforming to Rome. The Church in Rome had to remain close and focus on something much larger than the doomsday circumstances before them if they were to survive their panic of outside attack and internal turmoil (Philippians 2:1–5).

With worry and fear staring them in the face, the Church in Philippi was encouraged to keep their minds focused on what is more excellent in order to avoid anxiety. Paul gave a list of descriptors of things that would refocus their minds. His admonishment was to stop the repeat tracks of doomsday background music and start listening to what would refresh, renew, and refocus them in Christ.

> Finally, brothers, whatever is true, whatever is honorable, whatever is just, whatever is pure, whatever is lovely, whatever is commendable, if there is any excellence, if there is anything worthy of praise, think about these things (Philippians 4:8).

First, Paul said, focus on whatever is true.

Paul starts his list of new thinking by calling the Church's attention to what is true. The word *true* is defined as "describing something as credible, aligning with reality, reliable, or trustworthy."[1] Although Paul normally associates truth with the truth about God (Romans 1:18, 25) and truth of the Gospel of Christ (Galatians 2:5, 14; 2 Corinthians 4:2; 11:10), in the context of this list of virtues, he affirms whatever is true to be the only proper subject of Christian thought. Satan is the father of lies. Thinking on that which is false is to think the devil's thoughts, not God's thoughts.

Noble.

When I think of the word *noble*, I think of some British dignitary. That image is off, but close. Something noble is worthy of respect and honor. It is to be taken seriously and treated properly. Paul uses this word to describe the call or standard for godly older men (Titus 2:2), deacons (1 Timothy 3:8), and women (1 Timothy 3:11).[2]

Just.

When we think about what is *just*, we need to think about two expressions of justice: God's actions toward us and our actions of responsibility for God. "Just" has to do with God's standard of righteousness and the outplay of His righteousness among His people (Psalm 11:7).[3]

Pure.

In the original language, this word carries the idea that you are standing in awe of someone. This word is usually only attributed to God and communicates thinking on the holy purity of God. It has nuances of uncompromised integrity, which can only be found in God. When I dwell on what is pure, I am thinking about God's character—all of which is perfect and holy.

Pleasing.

What pleases your eye is what brings excitement and hope, not simply amusement. Children can be amused with an insect or rainbow, but it's the anticipation of Christmas Day or a birthday celebration where they truly delight in what they anticipate. Something pleasing is a source of joy for the downcast and is like a fragrance that fills the whole house like a batch of freshly baked chocolate chip cookies.

Commendable.

That which others look at with admiration is what we may refer to as *commendable*. These are the respectable things in life that others find joy and pleasure in and want to hear about or be around.

Paul lists these characteristics as the focal point for renewing our minds and giving us fighting power against anxiety. One commentator said, "Those who focus their minds on all that is true and set their minds and wills to do all that Paul has taught by word and example will experience the promise of the presence of the God of peace."[4] Grasping this kind of peace is the very thing that will move us from living on the defense against Satan and playing for the offense of God's Kingdom.

WATCH OUT FOR HYPERVIGILANCE

Police officers deal with the highs and lows that come from a constant state of hypervigilance. Their job demands them to look at life through the lens of defense, always being on the alert. What may be disturbing to us can trigger an internal reaction for them.

Is that guy reaching for his wallet or a weapon?

Is that a sound I hear behind me?

Are those guys following me?

Is she trying to get away with something?

The adage "bad guys don't wear name tags" causes cops to be on guard constantly. This is, in fact, what we expect them to do for us, but it means that they live a lifestyle of hypervigilance.[5]

Always being on alert can be taxing. In the right context, such as being an officer on duty, it can be energizing and even fun. However, when a hypervigilant person returns to their safe place and no longer has to be on the lookout, they often crash emotionally and even physically. This biological response can express itself as laziness, being downcast, or even anger. Cops are not the only ones who experience this hypervigilance. As a pastor, I feel it often. There are environments in my life—even in church—where I am hypervigilant. My wife will even say to our kids when I get home, "We know Daddy is home, but Daddy doesn't know he is home yet," because my mind is still coming down from the battle I was just in at work.

Hypervigilance may be what you are experiencing because of your racing thoughts. Your mind has you constantly on alert, and you can't seem to calm down. When you do calm down, your emotions plummet, and you don't feel like doing much of anything.

A hypervigilant life is no way to live. God meant for us to enjoy this world, not walk around it being afraid. Renewing our minds begins with letting go of all-consuming thoughts that keep our highs high and our lows deeper than we care to admit. When we're hypervigilant, our body plays into this by causing our hearts to race, palms to sweat, blood pressures to rise, and breathing to be shallow. When we come out of hypervigilance, we want to lie down. We can't go on like this—it's unhealthy for any period. By fixing our minds on what is worth our attention, we can train our outer bodies and inner souls to be still and trust God, even when fear threatens to disrupt our everyday lives.

DESTROY THE NEGATIVE TRACKS

Here are some very practical actions you can take to get the negative tracks to stop playing in your head:

Identify your negative tracks. You may need to write down what keeps replaying in your mind. Sometimes writing these things out and seeing them as they are can help you realize how ridiculous they are, or that they may be more imaginary than real.

Flip to the truth. I have sometimes taken a stack of three-by-five cards and written one anxious thought on each. On the opposite side of the card, I write down a Bible verse or a truth that counteracts that anxious thought. Then I take time each day to flip those cards over, one by one, letting the truth sink in more than the lie. Soon I find that my thinking is renewed and rewired to the truth whenever that anxious thought arises.

Speak them honestly. As I mentioned in Chapter 4, sometimes the darkest thoughts in our minds must be exposed to the fresh air of faith. We can be brutally honest with God about what's plaguing us. He can use our honesty as a means of transformation. There is nothing you can say to God that He doesn't already know or that He doesn't have the resources to address.

Focus on what is more beautiful. Thinking about what is more lovely may help us to get over the ugly thoughts that consume us. For me, this comes when I go hold a new baby, walk in the woods, sit on a high point and watch the sunset, or savor a beautifully crafted cappuccino. There are a billion overlooked blessings in your life right now that could refresh your focus. God's common graces can provide a way for you to get your eyes off yourself and on the goodness of God.

Worship in spirit and truth. God made us to worship. Even my dad, who hates to sing (and frankly is not that good at it), loves it when a room full of people raise their voices to God. My dad would drive in his 1994 Nissan Pathfinder with his Promise Keepers praise album blaring as he sang along. As a kid, I remember his sincere joy from worshiping God through some of our hardest times. On my best days and worst days, there is nothing like listening and singing to music that worships God to get my mind out of the rut it likes to run in. When we worship in spirit and truth, the lies we believe flee, and God stirs our souls to provide comfort and clarity.

Meditate on Christ. I remember my youth pastor saying, "Thirty seconds of thinking about Christ will cure the worst day and the strongest temptation." He was right. Simply stopping and thinking about Jesus Christ, His character, His grace, the cross, and His resurrection—these are the most beautiful things with which to fill our minds. A few seconds of thinking about Christ or reading Scripture about Him has a way of affecting the rest of my day.

Now is the time to roll down the window of your soul and let that mixtape of negative tracks unwind in the wind of God's truth. It's time you break up with those thoughts and keep your gaze firmly fixed on the Author and Perfecter of our faith—Jesus Christ (Hebrews 12:2).

THREE STEPS TOWARD THE END OF ANXIETY

ACT

Create your own stack of three-by-five cards as described in this chapter. Start replacing the lies you believe with the truths of Scripture and what you know about God and His perspective on your situation.

REFLECT

Are you living in a constant state of "hypervigilance" and living in fear more than peace?

MEMORIZE

Commit Romans 12:2 to memory and remember that you can renew your mind by the power of Christ working in you.

HOW CAN I MAKE THESE FEELINGS GO AWAY?

CHAPTER 9

CAN'T EAT, SLEEP, OR BREATHE? START HERE

START WITH SCRIPTURE
Genesis 15:1–6; Exodus 3:1–4:17

CORE PRINCIPLE NINE

It is possible to regain stability and find security, but it will only come by changing our motives, thinking, and behavior. Doing what you've been doing will only give you the same results.

Sarah Fader, a social media consultant in Brooklyn, made it clear that anxiety is now a generalized disorder for all. She texted her friend about coming to visit, but Sarah became uneasy when her friend didn't respond quickly. Sarah posted on Twitter to her sixteen-thousand-plus followers: "I don't hear from my friend for a day—my thought, they don't want to be my friend anymore." She appended the hashtag #ThisIsWhatAnxietyFeelsLike.

Her tweet and hashtag went viral. Thousands of people were soon sharing their examples under the same hashtag, with multiple responses retweeted thousands of times. Sarah's honesty ignited a powerful response. Chances are you resonate with that same type of gripping fear, and you may have your own anxiety-driven confession. That's the reality we all face because we are humans living in constant "on" culture.

The *New York Times* reported that our society has moved from being depressed to being anxious, as shared in the powerful article "Prozac Nation Is Now the United States of Xanax." Anxiety disorders are the number one mental disorder in America, affecting forty million adults in the United States aged eighteen and older—18 percent of the population every year. According to data from the National Institute of Mental Health, approximately 38 percent of girls and 26 percent of boys aged thirteen through seventeen suffer from some form of an anxiety disorder. On college campuses, anxiety is rampant and far outpacing depression as the most common mental health concern for undergraduates. The number of Google searches related to anxiety has doubled in the last five years, according to Google Trends.

Anxiety manifests in a multitude of ways: feeling distressed, uneasy, worried, upset, fearful, apprehensive, agitated, fretful, restless, nervous, and fidgety, to name just a few. Fear can be a symptom of anxiety or the cause of it. Fear and anxiety are different yet interrelated. "The difference between fear and anxiety is that fear is usually caused by tangible objects or threats. Anxiety picks up where fear leaves off and is mostly directed toward imagined or unrealized objects or conditions. Anxiety is more vague and more pervasive."[1]

ARE YOU HUMAN?

By this point in the book, you've probably openly admitted that you are dealing with anxiety, but take this self-assessment to gauge your current state right now. Answer either "Yes" or "No," giving the first answer that comes to mind.

	Yes	No
Is feeling "stressed" something you experience more than three days a week?		
Do you worry about your body often—be it because of your appearance and/or because you fear diseases or sickness?		
Do you spend more than a few moments a day thinking about bad things that happened to you in the past?		
Do you use alcohol, drugs, or pornography to escape the pressure you feel in life?		
Do you struggle with being easily irritable or find yourself having angry outbursts?		
Do you struggle with a racing heart, dizziness, shortness of breath, or sudden sweating in certain situations or after certain thoughts?		
Are there things you constantly do to calm yourself, such as check your phone, check the locks on the door, wash your hands repeatedly, etc., despite trying to resist?		
When you pray, do you find yourself only praying about possible bad situations rather than thanking God for the good things He has done?		
Are there places, people, or scenarios you avoid because you assume something bad will happen?		
Do you find it hard to fall asleep or to stay asleep at night?		
Do you worry about what people think of you?		

If you marked "Yes" to any one of those, then you deal with anxiety. Congratulations—you are human. If you marked more than five of those, anxiety is a pervasive problem in your life and is likely even hindering you from hearing and believing the promises of God. When worry and anxiety overtake you, it is hard to quiet them enough to hear what Jesus may be trying to say.

BE STILL, BUT HOW?

You may have seen this verse in a cross-stitch design hanging on your grandma's wall or printed on a coffee mug in a Christian bookstore: "Be still and know that I am God" (Psalm 46:10). The Sons of Korah wrote this in their well-quoted Psalm about God's being our fortress. Those guys had a rough lineage. God told everyone to stay away from them and then literally opened the earth to swallow their fathers (Numbers 16:28–35). Yet the sons of those rebellious fathers knew the power of God's redemption. Instead of living in fear that the earth would eat them too, they pressed into the presence of God. Perhaps the cure for their anxiety is found in the words they penned in some of the Bible's best hymns:

"As a deer pants for flowing streams, so pants my soul for You, O God" (Psalm 42:1).

"How lovely is Your dwelling place, O LORD of hosts" (Psalm 84:1).

"God is our refuge and strength, a very present help in trouble. Therefore we will not fear though the earth gives way, though the mountains be moved into the heart of the sea, though its waters roar and foam, though the mountains tremble at its swelling" (Psalm 46:1–3).

"Be still and know that He is God" may be one of their most widely quoted lines, but it is not so easily applied. The "know that

He is God" part is not the one our hearts argue against—it is the "be still" part with which we struggle. That's because we lack a depth of application to our knowledge of God that allows us to be still. When we "know God," we have a proper understanding (within our limitations) of who He is. But knowledge without application will lead to pride, not peace. When we act on what we know about God, the first necessary action (or reaction) is to *fear* God. It means we are in awe of what we have discovered about God. It is a sense of devotion to God because we are over-whelmed by His love, hope, and grace. The fear of God is the one "fear" that eliminates all other fears.

J. I. Packer, in his highly regarded book *Knowing God*, asks this probing question: "How can we turn our knowledge about God into knowledge of God? The rule for doing this is simple but demanding. It is that we turn each truth that we learn about God into matter for meditation before God, leading to prayer and praise to God."[2]

Truth is the key to battling anxiety. When we take what God has said about Himself and carve it into the walls of our heart, we loosen our grip on this world (or it loses its grip on us). Then we can hold tighter to the reality of who God is.

FEAR STARTS WITH AWE

Do you remember the first time you rode a roller coaster, saw the mountains, waded into the ocean, or held your child? You experience awe in exciting, meaningful first experiences. The feeling of awe swept you away, and you swore your life would never be the same. I want you to imagine for a moment feeling that same kind of excitement over your revelation of God. When you awake to the reality of a loving and gracious Creator, it causes your soul to experience awe for God.

Perhaps that feeling of awe for God never came for you, or maybe it is long past. What would it look like for you to have excitement and emotion over the Lord again?

You may be sitting there asking, "Can the fear of God really affect the anxiety and stress I have in my daily life?" The answer is yes. John Murray wrote, "The fear which frees us consists of awe. It is the reflex of our consciousness to the transcendent majesty and holiness of God."[3]

Here is a problem that plagues us all: Our awe of God is eclipsed by the anxiety in our lives. We worry about paying the bills. We worry about the future and the fulfilment of our dreams. We fret about the way we're raising our children. We feel stuck in a dead-end career. We struggle with marital conflicts. We are concerned that we're living a mediocre life rather than making meaningful contributions. All of these feelings distract us from looking at God and direct us to look only at ourselves. They are the symptoms of what author Paul David Tripp calls "Awe Amnesia." These symptoms mean we lack a right and "awe-filled" perspective of who God is and therefore end up with a relational and spiritually detrimental problem. When we lack the fear of God, we lack identity, purpose, and peace, which results in a gerbil-wheel of feelings that produce anxiety, worry, and panic. We must understand who God is *for us*. To that end, Tripp writes:

> [God] is awesome in power for us. He is awesome in sovereignty for us. He is awesome in mercy for us. He is awesome in wisdom for us. He is awesome in love for us. He is awesome in holiness for us. He is awesome in patience for us. He is awesome in faithfulness for us. He is awesome in grace for us. What He is, He is for us![4]

Only awe for God will keep our identity, self-image, and anxiety in their rightful places. Here is a truth to hold onto:

we will be in awe of what we believe will give us life (identity, meaning, purpose, pleasure). So, if we have what Tripp called "awe amnesia" and forget who God is, we lose sight of who we are. Then we nervously search the earth for something we've already received from Heaven.

FEAR OF GOD IS MADE POSSIBLE BY THE GOSPEL

At the church where I serve as pastor, we have a midweek staff chapel where we come together to worship Jesus and hear a short message from God's Word. We had one chapel around Christmastime that we affectionately referred to as "the crying chapel." I decided to teach on Isaiah 9:6, which says,

> For to us a child is born,
> to us a son is given;
> and the government shall be upon His shoulder,
> and His name shall be called
> Wonderful Counselor, Mighty God,
> Everlasting Father, Prince of Peace.

At the end of my teaching, I passed out a bowl full of little slips of paper. Each slip had a name of God mentioned on it from Isaiah 9:6, "Wonderful Counselor, Mighty God, Everlasting God, Prince of Peace." I told everyone to take the one they identified with the most at that point in their life and share why they selected it. For the remainder of our time together, story after story included descriptions like these:

"I chose 'Wonderful Counselor' because God walked us through a hard marriage season this year."

"Mine is 'Mighty God' because of the way He spared the life of my nephew."

"I picked 'Prince of Peace' because I've been so worked up over our finances, but God has provided. When I am lying in my bed at night, He comforts me and catches my tears before they hit the pillow."

"I love the name 'Everlasting Father,' because God has been the dad I always wished I had, and so much more."

Our staff members still joke about how we can't have "crying chapels" more than once a year because that one was so emotionally exhausting. But if you ask any of the people there, they will tell you that was one of the sweetest times we've ever shared.

The beautiful words of Isaiah 9:6 point us to the person of Jesus, the truth that He was born of a virgin, lived with us, died for us, and was raised for us. That is what makes Him Wonderful Counselor, Mighty God, Everlasting Father, and Prince of Peace. Without Jesus, we would not be able to know God, fear God, or have awe for God. The Gospel of Jesus Christ awakens our dead hearts, opens our blind eyes, imbeds faith within our hearts, and allows us to know God.

Knowing the character of God allows us to say with the apostle Paul, "Do not be anxious about anything" (Philippians 4:6). The word for "anxious" here can also be translated as "worry," but the command in the Greek is much more forceful. It can be read as forbidding the continuation of an action that is already ongoing. In other words—stop it! Paul essentially says, "Stop perpetually worrying about everything." It is the same Greek word we find in Matthew 6:25, which says, "Therefore I tell you, do not be anxious about your life, what you will eat or what you will drink, nor about your body, what you will put on. Is not life more than food and the body more than clothing?"

God knows that we are habitually concerned about the problems and difficulties of life. He knows that anxiety is an ongoing state for us. But when we worry, we are more prone to sin. We will fight to keep what we have or get what we want. When we worry, we struggle to trust God. When we do not hear His voice, we grow even more anxious.

In the summer of my greatest anxiety, I lost nearly thirty pounds in just two months. I couldn't eat, sleep, or sometimes breathe. My wife, biblical counselor, and friends watched over me when I thought there was no way out. The only way out was to renew my thinking and renew my awe for God. I had to "be renewed by the transformation of my mind" (Romans 12:2). To continue to self-deprecate was a form of pride—thinking more of myself and my problems than I ought (Romans 12:4).

If you find yourself as I did, lost and confused in the ocean of my own overwhelming emotions, then it is time to come back to the secure shore of God. Remember His character. Remember His power. Remember He is for you.

THREE STEPS TOWARD THE END OF ANXIETY

REFLECT

Where are you experiencing "awe amnesia" and forgetting the goodness of God in your life? Reflect on where God has shown you who He is and what you know to be true of Him. Now evaluate your current fears in light of what you already know about God and His goodness.

ACT

Write down which name of God you identify with the most from Isaiah 9:6—Wonderful Counselor, Mighty God, Everlasting Father, Prince of Peace—and why.

MEMORIZE

2 Timothy 1:7 reads, "For God gave us a spirit not of fear but of power and love and self-control."

CHAPTER 10

FIGHT FEAR WITH FEAR

START WITH SCRIPTURE
Daniel 12:1–4; 2 Timothy 1:7

CORE PRINCIPLE TEN
There are two kinds of fear: (1) fear of God and (2) fear of reasonable danger. Both types of fear demand that we cultivate awe for God that compels us to run to Him, not away from Him.

Fear is brutal, relentless, and has a way of rocking our world in a second.

Have you ever had a moment where your fear feels more real to you than reality itself? Have you found yourself caught in the *what-ifs* more than *what is*? Has your heart ever sunk so deeply you find it hard to breathe? When were you most afraid or anxious in your life? How did your body respond? How did your *soul* respond?

There was a moment I'll never forget when my suffering seemed almost unbearable. My fear was as thick as midnight darkness, but God shined His light through it.

I was physically at a conference in Tennessee, but my mind and heart just wanted to be at home in Colorado. Being mentally present as the presenter spoke seemed to be a fight I could not win. I finally decided to skip the sessions, go to the airport, and try to catch an early flight back. I was facing real fear. Although not a threat against my physical body, it was fear that seemed to wreck me emotionally. My anxiety grew so overwhelming that I eventually couldn't feel my hands or feet. My vision started to fade, and everything around me turned white. As my legs became limp, I staggered slowly past the check-in desks at the airport in Nashville.

Like a hurt, hunchbacked animal, I made my way to a secluded place to tend my wounds, pass out, or die. I found a small elevator waiting area, and there I collapsed on the cold, hard tile. My suitcase fell over beside me as if it was agonizing with me. It was the first time I ever experienced a full-fledged panic attack.

My wife was on the phone in my earbuds, but my faint memory only recalls her sounding like she was underwater. I remember hearing her call my name but not being able to respond. Fear gripped me by the jugular—I seemed to be moving between consciousness and unconsciousness.

I felt totally out of control. Anxiety has a way of invading your life, insisting that whatever you thought was true is now no longer true.

Anxiety is real, but it almost always lies to you. As we've already learned, anxiety doesn't have to win, even when it tells you it will. That's the lie straight from Satan, the father of lies.

That experience was one of the worst times I've ever suffered from anxiety, fear, and worry, but it wasn't the only time. Fear has had a timeshare on the property of my heart for as long as I can remember, and it finds its sneaky way to intrude on me weekly, if not daily. When fear drives you to anxiety, it causes you to be senseless because it fails to acknowledge that the God who cares for you is in complete control. Anxiety accomplishes nothing useful on its own. It serves no purpose—until you turn your worry and fear into a desire to grow your faith. You can choose to remain an anxious mess, or you can allow your fears to be a resolution for greater trust in God.

Anxiety didn't win over me that day. After the police found me, they called for paramedics to come and take me away. I was hauled out on a gurney to an ambulance waiting outside. As they placed me inside, through sobbing tears, I said, "Listen, I know God has me; I just don't feel it right now. Please don't take me! I want to go home."

One of the nurses, a sweet lady, said, "You are right, Josh. God has you. You need only be still." The nurse's name was Lynn, and I asked her if I could pray with her. She squeezed my hand tightly, and I started praying loudly between my sobs for God to calm my anxious heart.

Lynn eventually got on the phone with Molly and told her I was going to be OK. She said, "Molly, you've got a godly man here...Jesus has both of you in His powerful grip." Tears filled my eyes then and now as I recall her compassion and reassuring words. She seemed to be sent by God at that moment to remind me that His peace will win if I will be still and know that He is God.

A few months later, Molly and I returned to that airport in Nashville. We stood there among the busy travelers and prayed together, thanking God for being the One who calms us, heals us, and meets us in our deepest struggles.

When overcome by fear, I have made this my prayer. If you are afraid or are in a dark valley of life right now, maybe it can be yours as well:

"Father, I thank you that I have nothing to fear. You will keep me safe" (Isaiah 8:13 NLT).

Fear is nothing new, but it will neutralize your faith faster than any other emotion. Since the very beginning of humanity, fear has invaded the lives of people. While fear was not a part of God's original design, sin came into the world, and that guarantees you will experience suffering on this side of Heaven.

You've been told since you were a kid not to be afraid, yet even as a grown-up Christian, you can find reasons to be anxious and fearful. Anxiety and fear are closely related, even though they are not the same. When you have one, you often see the other. Anxiety comes mostly from worrying about what *could* happen, while fear is created out of a dread of what *will* happen.

Your fears will tell you that something else or someone else will win. But the truth is that God's way always wins. God always triumphs over the great tragedies of your past. He always conquers the confusing circumstances of your present, and He always fights for your faith in the future.

There was a man in the Bible who chose to trust God with his fear—past, present, and future. His name was Daniel. We meet him as a young man in the book of Daniel and journey with him well into his eighties by the end of it.

Daniel fought his fair share of fear and anxiety throughout his life. In Daniel 11:1–12:13, we meet him as an old man during the reign of the king who finally allowed Daniel's exiled people to return to Jerusalem and rebuild it. At that point, he was in his mid-eighties, but he lived through many moments of terror while exiled in Babylon before that passage (compare Daniel 2, 3, 5, 7:28, 10:7). His final words seem to increase with trust in God, but this kind can only come after wrestling the beast of fear countless times over his life and watching God win.

Whether it was after being summoned to interpret the king's scary vision of handwriting on the wall and deliver its terrifying message (Daniel 5), seeing his friends thrown into a fire (Daniel 3), or being thrown into a pit with hungry lions (Daniel 6), Daniel always trusted God with the outcome. His circumstances drove him to greater dependence on God, and in the end, he surrendered his future and the future of his people to the Lord.

All the moments of fear that Daniel experienced compelled him to depend more greatly on the God who holds the past, present, and future. God's way always wins!

God graciously gave Daniel the company of angels several times throughout his life (Daniel 6:22; 7:16; 8:15; 9:21; 10:10; 12:5). But whether angels were present or not, Daniel embodied a calming sense of God's total control over all circumstances.

Daniel used the strength given by God to speak strength to others. Look at verse 11:1, which says, *"And as for me, in the first year of Darius the Mede, I stood up to confirm and strengthen him."*

Even though Daniel struggled to understand the mysteries of God and lived with fear gripping his soul at times, he didn't let anxiety get in the way of encouraging others. Arguably the greatest lesson you can learn from Daniel's life is that when you are facing fear, you need to use the strength God gives you to strengthen others. This book was written as an encouragement to those in exile. Though you have not been "exiled" from your home country on earth, spiritually speaking, you live in the paranoia of daily life exiled from God. You are not in your final home yet, but while you wait for the day when you will be fully with the Lord, you can find strength in the promise that God is near, and He will win in the end.

When you face fearful circumstances or are suffocating in anxiety, you must trust that Christ will comfort you now and return for you in the future. He provides this comfort and hope through His Word, the Holy Spirit, other people, situations, and consistent prayer.

In my most anxious moments, I have found that God meets me through any one of these various channels of grace. Yet when I am comforted by God, it would be selfish and wrong if I bottled up what Christ gave me and kept it only for myself. In the worst moments, I've received random text messages and emails from people I rarely talk to telling me that they were praying. God used other believers to comfort me right when I needed it the most. There was nothing coincidental about it. I could share a hundred stories of thoughtful letters or even passing statements when God spoke comfort and strength to me through others. Daniel did this for those in exile with him, so I should do the same.

God is always present and always encouraging you, and He gives you what you need in Christ *so that* you can also pass it on to others.

The words of the Apostle Paul urge you to use what you received in Christ to comfort others. Hold on to these words from 2 Corinthians 1:4: "[Christ] comforts us in all our affliction, so that we may be able to comfort those who are in any affliction, with the comfort with which we ourselves are comforted by God." Use what comfort you have, even in your lowest moments, to comfort others. The comfort of Christ shown to others helps eradicate fear in you.

When it comes to fighting fear, I have found that my fear decreases when I give myself to help those who are fighting fear as big as mine, if not bigger. When I take my eyes off myself or my own consuming thoughts, I am much more alive and glorifying to God.

ENCOURAGEMENT STARTS WITH COURAGE

Famed World War II tank commander General George Patton said, "Courage is fear holding on a minute longer." If you give in to your fears, you are on the path to defeat. If instead you stand strong in spite of your fears, you are on the path to victory. You must never forget that you are not in the battle alone. With the power of God on your side, you cannot be defeated. With the comfort of Christ, you can be courageous.

Like Daniel, my strength comes from knowing that God's way always wins (11:29–45). I never have to guess or merely *bet* that God's way always wins; I know that nothing thwarts His plan. Nothing. This kind of certainty is the beginning of all wisdom (Proverbs 9:10), specifically fearing the Lord—not fearing our outcome.

Fear will try to grip your heart at times, but the key is not letting it conquer your heart. Biblical counselor and author Stuart Scott talks about two types of good fear:

The fear of God. You have a sense of "awe" for God that compels you to surrender to His way in your life fully. Fearing God is not the same as being afraid of God. When you are afraid of God, you run *from* Him; when you fear God, you run *to* Him. You are commanded in the Bible to fear God (Deuteronomy 13:4) and are told that this is the beginning of wisdom (Proverbs 1). When you have the right fear of God, you will be kept safe from wrong and ungodly fears.

Reasonable fears of danger or difficulty. As God's created being living in a fallen world away from Him, there are fears of danger and difficult circumstances that are reasonable.

Scott goes on to say, "God wants us to live in reality, but at the same time, He wants us to bring Him into the picture."[1]

You do have bodily responses to fear: adrenaline pumps through your veins, your muscles tense up, you get a dry mouth, wet pits, a pounding heart, and monster-sized butterflies in your stomach. These are responses to fear that God created. Fear is not wrong—what you do when you are afraid is what is important.

Daniel faced undeniable fear, but he responded to his fear with faith in God. His trust in God invited the presence of God. The angel even said to Daniel (10:12), "Fear not, Daniel, for from the first day that you set your heart to understand and humbled yourself before your God, your words have been heard, and I have come because of your words."

One of the greatest securities God can give you in the face of your fears is to know He hears you. When you humble yourself and trust God, He will hear you and come near (1 John 5:14; Psalm 66:19; 1 Peter 3:12).

However, just because God hears you doesn't guarantee that He is going to do things *your way*. The miracle you need may not be the miracle you are looking for during your trials. You need the miracle of Jesus Christ to remind you that you are broken, lost, and cannot be fixed in your strength. God is the One who says He will eradicate fear in your life and bring you home to be safe with Him.

If you believe that anything or anyone other than Jesus can fix you or eradicate your fears, then you will go to another person, place, or thing every time. It isn't until you believe that Jesus is the solution to your fear, worry, and anxiety that you will go straight to Him. That is where you will find the true and lasting solution your soul craves.

Your trials and pains may feel like immense losses. God wants to trade you joy for anxiety. He only allows you to go through the valley because He knows the mountain-peak blessing you will experience on the other side.

You may need to stop being afraid of the future and start clinging to the God who holds the future. Your past does not predict your future—only God does (Daniel 12:5–13). If you look to Christ, you can trust that you are not defined by your past failures; rather, your identity is found in the present and future reign of Christ (1 Corinthians 2:9). To be a Christian is to identify with Christ in His suffering and find healing in the redemptive power of forgiveness for your failures. You are not a "Past-ian," you are a "Christ-ian." Fears start to fade when you realize you are defined by who you are in Christ, not what you experienced in the past.

Whether you have days like I did in Nashville or are constantly living with a subtle fear of the future, I say to you: Don't sacrifice today on the altar of tomorrow. You don't know what tomorrow will hold; why let this day be ruined in fear of tomorrow?

Worship God alone and let your fear find rest in Him.

There are hundreds of "Fear not" statements in the Bible—both in narrative passages and in epistles. We can rest assured that God does not want His children to be gripped by fear merely by looking at the amount of times He addresses fear directly. Take your assurance in Christ, be clothed in His righteousness, and be comforted enough to turn around and comfort others. Be fearless and help others become the same.

THREE STEPS TOWARD THE END OF ANXIETY

REFLECT

Identify what fears you may be exaggerating in your mind and ask a friend to help you see the reality of your situation.

READ

Look up James 4:13–17. Write a paragraph of what this passage means for your life today. Where are you boasting in your own plans? Where are you worrying about the future that you can't control?

DISCUSS

Ask a friend to listen to your anxious thoughts and ask them to help you see where God is working positively, despite your negative thoughts. Evaluate with a friend where your fears are reasonable and where they are unreasonable and need to be corrected in light of trusting God.

CHAPTER 11

REMEMBER WHO YOU ARE (AND WHO YOU ARE NOT)

START WITH SCRIPTURE
John 15:1–11; 2 Timothy 1:6–7

CORE PRINCIPLE ELEVEN
God's steadfast love for me is true even when He allows suffering in my life. The pain I am going through is making me more like Christ and securing my identity in Him.

Anxiety and identity are linked. We may perceive that anxiety is tied to circumstances and surface-level issues only.

It's not.

Anxiety is felt so deeply because it bubbles up from our deepest places. If we do not have a clear understanding of who we are—or if we forget it for a season—then we will find ourselves fighting for security.

The longing for security starts long before we can even cognitively conceive it. As babies, we quickly learn who to trust and who not to trust. We can't even form a thought, let alone coherent words, but we can form a feeling or sense of security—or lack thereof. The attachment we feel early in life, usually first to our mothers, is the very bond-forming of our security in subsequent years.

Just as we form a sense of safety when we're young, we also form a spiritual identity in our first years of following Christ. Once we are reborn in faith, we grow in our understanding of who we are now as we are made new in Christ.

I've spoken to many Christians who explain their most vibrant years of faith as the first few years after trusting in Christ. These years are energizing because we discover our old self is fading away. There is forgiveness for our past. We have power in the present. Most importantly, we have the promise of living with God for all of eternity in the future.

As we continue in our relationship with Christ, the new-Christian smell wears off, and the truths that awakened us almost become too familiar. The Bible we couldn't put down is not picked up enough, and the excitement we felt when engaging in worship, church, or study seems to be more of a duty than delight. Why the change? Because we lost the joy of our salvation and forgot who we are in Christ. We start believing our identity is something other than God's very own.

We start giving ourselves new identities that are far less important or impressive than being called a child of God. Our identity statements are things like...

I am anxious.

I am depressed.

I am a wreck.

I am not worth anything.

I am hopeless.

We forget the beautiful identity given to us through Christ's sacrifice, and we allow new labels to tell the world who we believe we are and what we should feel. I get it—I'm not pointing fingers here. I am a pastor, so one would think I know my identity in

Christ more than most. The truth is that there are times when I, too, have wondered who I am. I've allowed what I feel or what someone tells me I am to be more real than who God says I am in Christ.

If you stare in the mirror long enough, you may start to wonder who's looking back at you. Even in my adult years, I have looked at my face in the mirror as if I am having a staring contest with the downcast version of myself. *Who are you? Why do you exist? When will everyone else see you're a fraud?* These questions can feel very weighty and steal the joy of knowing who I am in Christ.

WOULD THE REAL ME PLEASE STAND UP

At the counseling center I founded, we have a set of questions on the intake form that every guest is required to complete. The first of two questions that I believe are the most revealing is this: *People who know me think that I am* _____.

The question immediately following is this: *If they knew the "real me," they would know that I am* _____.

The answers to the first question are staggering to read. For many of our cases, people will write things such as "confident," "level-headed," "a servant," "happy and kind," "driven," "mature," "organized," "persevering," or "a planner."

These answers have similarities and reveal the deeper identity issues we all can become good at disguising. The second question's answers are where the cold reality comes to light as people write things like: "a control freak," "jealous," "insecure," "sinful," "anxious," "depressed," "lazy," "selfish," "confused," and even "lost."

Most of us are embarrassed to have people know the *real* us. We grow anxious about not meeting others' expectations or even our own. If there's nothing else you gain from this book other than this soul-soothing, heart-calming truth, I want you to know **there** is nothing you can do to make God love you more. There is nothing you can do to make God love you less.

He loves you,

because He loves you,

because He loves you,

because He loves you,

because He loves you,

because He loves you,

because He loves you,

because He loves you,

because He loves you,

because He loves you...because it is His indelible, immovable, undeniable nature to love you.

He loves all the way, all the time. His love is unchanging.[1]

So even if the *real* you is showing, God loves you. Pastor and author Matt Chandler told the story of how his wife says to him, "Your ugly is showing..." but follows with, "But I love you anyway!"

1 John 3:1 says, "See what great love the Father has lavished on us, that we should be called children of God! And that is what we are!"

Imagine if you started walking around saying, "Hi, I am the real _____. I am a mess, but my security is not in who I am but who Christ has made me to be. Nice to meet you." This response would not only create conversation, but it might start our relationships off on the right foot. We are not here to impress; we are here to experience the love of Christ and show His love to others.

Anxiety can be paralyzing, and our sense of inadequacy can breed fear or timidity and hinder God's work in our lives. We are called to actively develop our reliance on Christ because, in Christ, we already have the "spirit...of power and love and self-control." Paul put this all together for us in 2 Timothy 1:6–7: "For this reason

I remind you to fan into flame the gift of God, which is in you through the laying on of my hands, for God gave us a spirit not of fear but of power and love and self-control."

LIVING WITH YOUR HEART WIDE OPEN

I've spent extensive time studying Saint Augustine of Hippo. This man lived around 400 A.D. and was not afraid to "let his ugly show." That is one of the reasons I love him. He knew who he was in Christ and let go of who he was not. Augustine said it well: "Thou hast made us for thyself, O Lord, and our heart is restless until it finds its rest in thee." We rest and trust in the work of God and enjoy His presence as our source of security as He works in us.

The best biblical term for this idea of finding wellbeing in Christ while God works on us is "to abide." We see it mentioned most explicitly in John 15:1–11. What does abiding or remaining in Christ mean? It gives us a picture of remaining connected to God as our source of security. There is a divine sap running between the vine and the branches; it is the Holy Spirit. Abiding in Christ is parallel with being filled with the Spirit. Jesus said He would go so a greater one could come. The "greater" descriptor referred to magnitude, not hierarchy. All Christians, all over the world, can be connected to the same source of spiritual security at the same time and never run out of supply.

Some theologians will refer to the Holy Spirit as the "Alter Christos"—the other Christ, like Christ, but better for us. He is in us, helping us, holding us, securing us, and sealing us.

I love the Old Testament imagery of being "hidden" (or abiding) in God: "For He hid me in His shelter in His day of trouble...." (Psalm 27:5) and "He hid me in the shadow of His Hand..." (Isaiah 49:2). The calling to abide is a promise of provision, comfort, and guidance.

The real fruit of our characters comes with a deep connection to the vine of Christ. That is why God does not shield us from the assaults of this life, but rather exposes us to them so that we will learn to hold fast to Him.

Jesus said, "I am the Vine," but the Father is the Vinedresser (John 15:2, 6–7). As if to say, "I will give you what you need for life, but My Father is sovereignly in control of all life." Yes, there may be hardships (heat, wind, fire, flooding) in this life, but He will care for you and watch over you. The stressful and overwhelming trials we face are used by God to tether our dependence to Him. This is "dressing the vine"—weeding out what must go and strengthening what needs to remain.

One of the times I remember the Father tending to the branches in my life was when I was living in Chicago. I worked at a church where it seemed everything was going wrong. Poor leadership choices led to massive emotional chaos for many of us. It was during a time when I felt nothing but loss: loss of family, loss of friends, and eventually a loss of job and loss of clarity. I ended up packing up my apartment in the northwest suburbs of Chicago and driving a small U-Haul back to Denver. I was feeling nothing but loneliness, fear, confusion, and even anger. In all of this, God was "cutting away" what needed to be cut to bear more fruit.

I have learned there are two types of cutting away that happen by the Vinedresser:

Branches that are not bearing fruit. These are people who do not know Him. They claim to know Jesus Christ, but they are unfaithful and unfruitful. This type of cut is God's response to fruitlessness, as mentioned in John 15.

Branches that are bearing fruit. Even the branches that are doing well, those that best convey the life of the vine, get the knife. I have seen many faithful Christians get pruned.

I can get my head around the first type of cutting away, but why would He cut what's bearing some fruit? Some fruit is not necessarily better than no fruit, spiritually speaking, but God is in the business of *maximizing* our impact on the world for the Gospel of Christ. He's not satisfied with only *some* fruit; He deserves and calls out our greatest fruit of faithful living. For us to have maximum fruit production, He may allow cutting (suffering, pain, loss) to help the remaining parts of our lives be even more fruitful for Him.

WHAT'S INVOLVED IN PRUNING?

Pruning is when God is working through our circumstances and relationships to make us more like Christ. This deepens our faith and grows our identity as a trusting child of God. Let's call it what it is, though: pruning always hurts. Sometimes the pain of pruning is because of our sins or the result of someone else's sin. The bad has got to go, and at times, the good must go too to produce the better.

King David, a man after God's heart, was "pruned" so he could be more fruitful. Psalm 119:67 says, "Before I was afflicted I went astray, but now I keep Your word." And Psalm 119:71 says, "It is good for me that I was afflicted, that I might learn Your statutes." David acknowledged that his affliction was allowed by God, and it was for the better.

While pruning involves pain, it also always involves God's presence. God's hand is never closer than when He is pruning our hearts and lives.

PRUNING FROM GOD IS THE KEY TO YOUR TRANSFORMATION

God sometimes leads us through challenges and pain to increase our spiritual growth through tests of faith or trials of character. We may not be able to control what happens to us, but we can control our responses.

These responses to pruning will open our hearts and lives to a powerful transformation at the hands of our loving Heavenly Father:

Gratitude over grumbling: Recognize the love of the Father—if He didn't care, He wouldn't encourage growth.

Humility over haughtiness: Submit to the Lord's timing—this is the ultimate "trust Dad because He knows what He's doing."

Compassion over comparison: Use your pain to comfort others—few situations bring as fresh a perspective as pain and difficulty can.

Application over apathy: Press on to know God in the midst of discipline—you can't know the whole story if you stop reading in the middle.

Accountability over isolation: Involve the community in your growth process—yes, misery loves company, but even more so, transformation thrives with accountability.

Hope over despondency: Trust the unseen purpose of God. His plans are designed to give us hope in the end—even when we can't see or understand what it looks like to be at the end.

All members of the military begin their training with boot camp—the infamously intense stint of sweat and suffering by which they're made fit for military service. If the experience is as horrific as it's often portrayed in popular media, why do so many *voluntarily* put themselves through boot camp?

For one thing, boot camp is for a limited time. Although it is intense and perhaps brutal, it does not last forever. Once the training is complete, a season of reprieve will come. Secondly, the strength and ability gained through the training are that much greater because of its intensity. In other words, the outcome is worth the experience.

Similarly, the Christian can endure discipline knowing that the Lord ordained seasons of trial that will eventually end and lead to redemption (1 Peter 5:5). We can anticipate deeper, richer, and more lasting growth as we trust the Lord through a season of discipline. Our Heavenly Father is zealous for fruit from His vine, but producing it will often require deeper pruning than we would ever choose for ourselves. But it is worth it!

Abiding (or remaining) in Christ must not be reduced to a subjective, mystical, inner state. The mark of an abiding heart is not only, or even principally, a sense of inward serenity, but a "conscience clear before God and man" (Acts 24:16). It is allowing Jesus's words to remain in us as we cling to Him.

Because of God's "precious and very great promises" (1 Peter 1:4) secured in Christ, we can trust He will never leave or forsake us (Hebrews 13:8). He knows what we need even before we ask Him (Matthew 6:8), and as we commit ourselves to Him, He will complete His good work in us (Philippians 1:6). He only asks for us to trust—to abide!

When we remain in Christ and keep our identity fixed on Him, our lives will be hidden in Christ and become a display of God's glory for the world. Colossians 3:3 says, "For you have died, and your life is hidden with Christ in God." Every part of my heart aches to be hidden and abide in Him and find true life there, not in my whirlwind of anxiety and emotions!

WHEN DID YOU FEEL GOD'S PRUNING?

I want you to reflect on the past twelve months. Can you identify any experience of discipline in your life? How did God bring a harvest out of the pruning? If you can identify the harvest, take time to give thanks to God, reaffirm your trust in His loving care over your life, and consider how your experience equipped you to better participate in God's mission.

Did you learn from your past pruning, or did you slough it off as circumstance and miss what God had for you to learn? How are you applying what you learned?

If you are in the midst of a pruning season and cannot yet see the fruit, I want you to read and meditate on Psalm 13. The Psalmist, being in profound anguish, nevertheless expressed deep, abiding trust in God. Maybe right now, you need to honestly talk to God about the battle you are in to trust Him and ask for His help in remaining faithful.

We can have hope and gratitude knowing that even the Apostle Paul called his sufferings "light momentary affliction," which is itself "preparing for us an eternal weight of glory beyond all comparison" (2 Corinthians 4:17).

Again, the hand of God is never closer than when He is pruning you. Breathe deeply and exhale slowly. Let your nostrils release the anxiety, fear, and even doubt pressure-packed in your soul—and breathe slowly again. Allow your roots to deepen in your security in Christ. Anxiety and identity are linked, but this can be to your benefit as your identity in Christ eclipses your emotions.

Someday we will be face-to-face with the One who carved our beings into existence and prunes our hearts and lives to bear more fruit today. I can't wait for the day when I see my Savior's face.

THREE STEPS TOWARD THE END OF ANXIETY

REFLECT

Address lifestyle rhythms that may be influencing or intensifying your anxiety. Choose one or two areas of your daily life, such as your diet, sleep, work schedule, recreational time, or exercise, and make a manageable goal to change that area. For example: "I will work out after work for forty-five minutes three times this week," or "I will try to get at least seven hours of sleep a night." Pruning can involve changing your daily rhythms.

ACT

Write out your life purpose in one sentence. Don't overthink it. What is the unique purpose God has placed you on this earth to fulfill? Is your purpose compelling you to serve Christ and others in the future rather than worrying about failures of the past?

MEDITATE

In Christ, God is for us (compare Romans 8:31–34). List twelve ways you know this is true in your life now.

CHAPTER 12

AVOID ANXIETY'S EVIL COUSIN, DEPRESSION

START WITH SCRIPTURE

Matthew 14:22–33; Lamentations 3:1–26

CORE PRINCIPLE TWELVE

Depression and anxiety are closely related and often experienced as a one-two punch to our hearts. Having the right perspective is essential for fighting and overcoming both through the power of Jesus and the peace of the Holy Spirit.

ir. I needed air. Despair trapped my heart and clenched its fingers around my throat. I punched in the numbers and made the call.

My wife, Molly, was at a prayer meeting, and I'd just finished putting our kids to bed. My parents knew I wasn't doing well and answered my call to come over so I could go for a walk. They could hear it in my voice when they answered; no explanation was needed.

Dad offered to go on the walk with me, not wanting me to be unaccompanied.

"No, I'll be fine—please stay at the house with the kids. I need to be alone."

My dad's words telegraphed his concern.

"Joshua, take my phone, so I can know where you are...and that you're OK."

My dad is one of the few people who call me by my full name. Most people know me as Josh. The congregation under my care knows me as Pastor Josh.

At that moment, I wasn't anyone else but *Joshua*.

At that moment, I knew the darkness outside was nothing compared to the darkness clouding my soul in depression.

That summer, my all-too-familiar opponent—depression—was ready for another round. It seems to pop up at the worst times, but let's be honest: there's never a good time for depression. It haunts me when deadlines are looming, the kids are off at school, family gatherings are planned, and the moments that matter are right in front of me.

Those things were all true at that moment as I left for my walk.

I walked to a path that winds around the open space near our house, where our family often walks during the summer. My body was hunching over more and more with every step under the crushing pressure of depression. Eventually, I dropped to the ground and lay on the path in tears.

Nothing. Nothing but darkness and my cries. I don't know how long I lay there, sobbing in my darkness, begging for God to let me die.

"God, isn't this enough?" I cried. "Make it stop, *please!*"

I repeated those words more times than I can remember. Some time later, I found the strength to get back up and walk home.

That night was dark for many reasons. My hope was bleak, and God seemed silent. What I couldn't see was that God was doing something—*He's always up to something*. He was producing something in me that could not come any other way.

God was teaching me to trust Him even when all I wanted to do was lay down and die.

Depression has a way of making you feel like you are living underwater...in the dark...with *something* stalking you in the waves, baring its teeth for the next attack as your body shakes in fear and panic.

I've lain awake at every hour of the night crying into my pillow so my wife and kids wouldn't hear me. I've gagged down the sound of my wails, terrified at what that sound would do if they heard how Daddy was *really* doing.

Only the weight of pure exhaustion causes my tears to stop— and that's when the next terror hits. Every one of my limbs feels like a hundred pounds, pinning me to the mattress and paralyzing my mind and heart.

Over the years, depression has surrounded me like a suffocating fog, not lifting or breaking for months on end. I have been a pastor for fourteen years now. I bet if you had asked me two decades ago if pastors could get depressed, I would have told you, "No way!" In fact, I bet I would have tried to preach a mini-sermon on why Christians, let alone pastors, have no reason to be depressed.

That was ignorance, and I recognize it now because you can't truly understand depression unless you've personally fought that darkness.

Christian culture has a way of offering nothing but clichés to address this severe problem. If those don't work, deep sadness is met with a "just snap out of it" reaction from those who have not fought this fight.

Even the most well-meaning, loving people in our lives don't know what to do when they see us wrestling with depression. I can't blame them; a person drowning under the severe waves of sadness has little hope of catching any life raft thrown their way. What can anyone else do to help?

Depression can be destructive, negative, even demonic. But the chief end of all things, including our emotions, is to bring glory to

God. While none of us would wish to have depression as a part of our lives, we need to recognize how God uses this terror of terrors to show us more of Christ.

If you deal with anxiety, then certainly you've met its evil cousin, depression. It's thrown its gut-punches at you, and you understand its suffocating power. Yet you still hold on to hope that there is relief around the corner.

MEET THE WEEPING PROPHET: JEREMIAH

There is a man who spoke on behalf of God in biblical history who was known for his weeping. What a reputation, right? He had his fair share of public crying sessions, which certainly were only a percentage of the time he spent crying to God in a disparaging tone on his own.

Jeremiah had good reasons for gaining the reputation of being a weeper. The time he lived in was full of tragedy and sadness. The king of Judah at that time, Zedekiah, decided to rebel against Babylon around the ninth year of his reign. King Nebuchadnezzar of Babylon advanced against Jerusalem and began a siege that finally led to the downfall of the city and the end of the Judean monarchy in July 586 B.C. (2 Kings 25:1–7). Forced to flee for his life as the city fell, Jeremiah was captured near Jericho and brought to Nebuchadnezzar's headquarters near Riblah. There, Zedekiah's sons were slain before him, and his own eyes were cut out. There were unspeakable things done in that holy city.

This city, Jerusalem, was where the first Temple was built by Solomon—the physical place God chose to dwell on earth with His children, His creation. The people disobeyed God, and God allowed destruction, though He never stopped being their God. So His chosen people were deported to Babylon. Not only was there physical destruction, but there was spiritual destruction as well. Are you beginning to see why Jeremiah was a wreck?

They were a captured people who lost everything, and depression flooded their hearts. They were as distraught and downcast as you can imagine anyone could be. In addition to the stories the Bible tells us about this time, some Psalms talk about widespread death, hopelessness, the thriving of enemies, and starvation so bad that people cannibalized their children.

Lamentations is a book written—most likely by Jeremiah— about what it was like living in that time. Upset with God and in despair emotionally, Jeremiah penned these words:

> He has made my teeth grind on gravel,
> and made me cower in ashes;
> my soul is bereft of peace;
> I have forgotten what happiness is;
> so I say, "My endurance has perished;
> so has my hope from the LORD"
> (Lamentations 3:16–18).

Look at what Jeremiah said: he had "forgotten what happiness is," and even his hope for the Lord ran out. In case there's any doubt, this is the face of depression.

Why would God allow this kind of feeling? Let's be clear: Depression was not in God's original design in Genesis 1. Depression exists because of sin, and it is a form of suffering. The reason Jeremiah is speaking like this is because of the evil done to him and around him.

When someone dealing with depression comes into our counseling office, we quickly identify *together* if the circumstances causing depression are caused by the effects of sin in and around us. I do not believe that depression is a sin, but depression is caused by sin in the world, and it can further propagate sin in our lives if we allow it. In God's perfect plan, we were meant to live with Him, which would have given us total access to His love, joy, and peace.

We need Jesus, especially in our most desperate situations. He gives us access to return to the relationship that will lift the dark cloud of depression once and for all.

SIN WARPS OUR PERSPECTIVES, BUT CHRIST BRINGS CLARITY

It's a miracle that everyone on earth does not walk around in a state of depression and with constant panic attacks. The world is a wicked and depraved place, and our only hope of a positive outward perspective is to know that God is still in control.

Christ changes our perspective by changing us. He makes us a "new creation" and gives us a renewed state before God and a renewed mind in this world (Romans 12:2). While we may still deal with feelings of depression from circumstantial sadness, fatigue, grief, imbalanced hormones, or stress, all of us can have a changed perspective with the hope of Christ.

Reacting to life's events with sadness may be the only right response for some things—but that doesn't mean you should stay there and resist change. *Reactive resistance* is the emotion we feel as a *reaction* to something that has happened (or not happened) in our lives, and it is *resistance* to life, help, or hope—even for God (see Romans 3:18). Even those who face physiological challenges and find themselves depressed must be open to help from God and the common graces of this world to pull them through. Those of us who deal with seasons of being "down" or "distraught" must push through to find Christ's power to change our perspective.

I like the way my friend Daniel Henderson says that disappointment is a temporary loss of perspective. Being a Christian and being depressed are two realities that will fight each other. Following Christ will mean hardship, but it also promises joy and peace.

NOT ALONE

Imagine being invited to a dinner party where these people were on the guest list: Abraham Lincoln, Theodore Roosevelt, Robert Schumann, Ludwig van Beethoven, Edgar Allan Poe, Mark Twain, Vincent van Gogh, and even Charles Spurgeon, C.S. Lewis, Barbara Bush, and Mother Teresa. When you arrive, Schumann and Beethoven are discussing the movements in their most recent musical compositions, Poe and Twain are listening to van Gogh talk about the meaning of his art, Roosevelt and Lincoln are discussing politics, Spurgeon and Lewis are discussing the Church of England, and Mother Teresa and Barbara Bush are expressing their love for children to each other.

You wonder why these people are here. After all, this is a fundraiser to help people suffering from depression. Maybe they all have someone in their family who suffers from depression. The time arrives during the dinner for speeches by special guests. You are shocked as one by one, each of these famous people describes his or her personal battle with depression. Lincoln takes the stage and begins by saying, "Several years ago, I wrote this in a letter to a friend," and reads:

> I am now the most miserable man living. If what I feel were equally distributed to the whole human family, there would be not one cheerful face on earth. Whether I shall ever be better, I cannot tell. I awfully forebode I

shall not. To remain as I am is impossible. I must die or
be better; it appears to me.[1]

Lincoln encourages everyone to persevere, for he says that he
wrote this in another letter some years later:

> The year that is drawing toward the close has been filled
> with the blessings of fruitful fields and healthful skies.
> These bounties are so constantly enjoyed that we are
> prone to forget the source from which they come.

When faced with depression, we must *choose to remember* the
goodness in life and that God is the source from which goodness
comes. We must humble ourselves and seek God to help us, and then
we will experience the power of a changed life and perspective.

Jeremiah, at his wits' end, finally bows and begs God for help
in Lamentations 3:19–20, saying, "Remember my affliction and
my wanderings, the wormwood and the gall! My soul continually
remembers it and is bowed down within me."

Many other biblical examples support the idea that depression
can result simply from living in a broken world. Psalms 10, 43, 69,
and 88 ask questions like: "Why are you downcast, oh my soul?"
A passage that may prove decisive in the debate contains the words
of Jesus Himself in Matthew 26:38: "My soul is very sorrowful,
even to death."

Lamentations models for us that there are no easy words in the
face of agony. It was a time of uncertainty, and the poet does not
allow that uncertainty to be resolved by easy words. The future
would be determined by the character and purposes of God.

Likewise, along with Job, the Psalms, and Ecclesiastes, the themes
of Lamentations indicate to us that expressing grief and sadness
are appropriate for the believer. Lamentations 3:20 intensifies the

negative memory with the typical Hebrew structure by saying the same thing twice: "remembering, my soul remembers…" In other words, "I vividly, frequently, painfully, wretchedly, continually remember…" until my soul sinks into misery and depression.

The lesson for us is this: we can face bad memories and emotions, but we must quickly transition to trusting the goodness of God.

While depression may not be a sin, it is caused by sin in the world. This means that we will experience things we try to forget, yet these memories can plague us for life. However, we can trust God and His character to help us overcome the emotions associated with those memories.

Whether depression is caused by physical, emotional, or spiritual realities, and whether it is spontaneous or caused by a terrible circumstance, we can recall God's character even in the midst of it.

Look at how the author of Lamentations changes his perspective once he turns to God:

> But this I call to mind, and therefore I have hope: The steadfast love of the LORD never ceases; His mercies never come to an end; they are new every morning; great is Your faithfulness. "The LORD is my portion," says my soul, "therefore I will hope in Him." The LORD is good to those who wait for Him, to the soul who seeks Him. It is good that one should wait quietly for the salvation of the LORD (Lamentations 3:21–26).

Depression has one main solution: trusting in God. We are told to trust in the Lord over and over and over in the Bible. We trust in the Lord because He and He alone is truly trustworthy. His plans for us are perfect and purposeful (Isaiah 46:10; Jeremiah 29:11).

God's character demands that I wait on Him. By waiting on God, I will have a fearless and faithful life. Your feelings of depression may be the very things God is using to call you to a deeper faith in Him. God brings us to a place where we must wait on Him, and it is so loving for Him to do so.

In moments of depression and anxiety, it can feel like God is nowhere to be found, and we grow frustrated and discouraged. No one wants to have to beg for something, especially from God. *Why won't He answer me?* Sometimes we would rather Him say something, even if it is not the answer we want. But to say nothing stings worse.

King David understood this feeling. He screamed at God in the Psalms when he said, "Answer me, O God! My spirit fails me! Hide not Your face from me, lest I be like those who go down to the pit" (Psalm 143:7). Done with waiting and on the edge of depression, he essentially said, "If You don't start talking, You might as well send me to Hell, because this is equivalent to the worst punishment ever."

When God goes silent in our pain, loneliness and loss set in. We have two choices at that point: Will we allow our bitterness to grow, or will we allow our trust in Him to deepen?

C.S. Lewis said it well after the loss of his beloved wife, Joy, when he wrote:

> God has not been trying an experiment on my faith or love in order to find out their quality. He knew it already. It was I who didn't. In this trial He makes us occupy the dock, the witness box, and the bench all at once. He always knew that my temple was a house of cards. His only way of making me realize the fact was to knock it down.[2]

Allowing the Lord to knock down your house of cards may be the best thing that happens to you. Depression won't win; God will.

THREE STEPS TOWARD THE END OF ANXIETY

READ

Study the whole book of Philippians at least one time through. Take note of how we are to have joy in all circumstances.

MEMORIZE

Commit to memory Job 13:15, which says, "Though he slay me, I will hope in him; yet I will argue my ways to his face."

ACT

Make a "think and do" list of profitable things you can *think* and *do* when you are feeling down to lift your heart and redirect your focus back on God. (Hint: keep the list with you for quick reference.)

HOW WILL MY LIFE BE BETTER IN THE END?

CHAPTER 13

FORGIVE MUCH BECAUSE YOU HAVE BEEN FORGIVEN MUCH

START WITH SCRIPTURE
Colossians 2:13 and Ephesians 4:32

CORE PRINCIPLE THIRTEEN
Dealing with anxiety demands that I find healing from Christ for my sin and begin healing from the hurt caused by others.

Warning: this is a gritty, messy, open-heart-surgery-style chapter. It's not supposed to be polished and picture-perfect because forgiveness rarely is.

Forgiveness is sticky and unpredictable. It hurts, especially when the person you're forgiving is indifferent about his or her need for forgiveness. It's a hard topic to write about, but it's even harder to live out.

When someone hurts us, it's harder to forgive than to resent. We feel justified in holding on to hurt because it shines the spotlight on our pain—I'm the victim, which also makes me the debt collector! It sounds horrible to admit, but it's true. How would I know? Been there, done that, and have the scars to prove it.

Forgiveness can feel as though we're being told to forget what someone did to us, and frankly, we can't forget. Correction: we don't *want* to forget. In some cases, the pain is too severe to let go that easily.

Now I want to be *very* clear: there are some situations, some wrongs, even horrific atrocities that happen in our world—maybe even in your own life—that are so bad they make simply the idea of forgiving them unimaginable. As a pastor, husband, father of five, and a broken, sinful man myself, I want you to know that forgiveness is *still* within your control.

Never let anyone force or shame you to forgive before the Holy Spirit moves your heart to grasp the full gravity of forgiveness. Forgiveness is not easy, free, or cheap. It costs something. You need the Holy Spirit's help. You are the one carrying the burden of forgiveness alone, which is too much for anyone to bear.

I wouldn't be much of a pastor if I encouraged you to follow the Spirit's timing without also advising you to be careful. Pain, anger, bitterness, and resentment are natural predators that, if you hold on to them, *will* eat you alive if you're not careful. When you don't forgive, your soul is in danger of becoming permanently scarred. While the wrongdoer may go on as if nothing happened, you're dying inside.

No conversation about forgiveness is complete without acknowledging our own need for forgiveness. Without sin, there would be no reason for forgiveness. The Gospel of Jesus Christ reminds us that the doctrine of forgiveness is at the core of Christianity. We sinned against God (and others) and need forgiveness.

Withholding our forgiveness is to suggest we have nothing for which to be forgiven. We forgive because God forgave us in Christ. The only way to be right with God is by His forgiving our sins, which He granted through the death and resurrection of His Son (Colossians 2:13). Jesus reconciles us with God and enables us to forgive those who sin against us.

THE DIFFERENCE BETWEEN BEING FORGIVEN AND FORGIVING OTHERS

Anxiety will remain present in your life if there is unconfessed personal sin and unforgiveness toward others. Forgiveness is a necessary elixir for a sick heart, whether it is caused by our sinfulness or the sinfulness of others. We need to look at forgiveness from two different angles if we're going to overcome anxiety over what happened in our pasts.

First, we must accept our forgiveness from God and others.

Second, we must grant forgiveness to those who hurt us.

I have had severe anxiety over two types of hurts. There are self-inflicted wounds that I needed to confess and ask forgiveness for, and then there are wounds from others that I must forgive. Without a proper understanding of forgiveness, it's impossible to grant or accept the biblical prescription for dealing with past pain.

FORGIVENESS STARTS WITH RELEASE

One of the Bible's key themes of forgiveness is the idea of *release*. The most common word for forgiveness in the Bible is ἀφίημι—which means "*release.*" It occurs 280 times in the Septuagint and New Testament. The word has the root meaning "from" and carries the idea of being "released from one's presence,"[1] or "released from legal or moral obligation or consequence."[2] There is a finality to this word as if all outstanding issues were settled. Forgiveness is releasing someone from the claim of moral debt and releasing your need for repayment or restitution. Forgiveness involves canceling a debt and letting the offender go free, no longer owing anything.[3]

That all sounds great, but let's bring it into a real-life, you-and-me context. We both have sinned against God in different ways at different times. Sin against an eternal God deserves eternal punishment. It's a terminal infection of our hearts that only forgiveness from God can cure.

When we place our faith in Christ, we are granted true forgiveness—the antidote for our infection of sin. It is a release of the punishment we deserve. Christ is our propitiation, John says (1 John 2:2), which means that Christ appeased the wrath of God that we deserve. Any sin we commit needs first to be confessed to God. Because of Christ, we can rest assured that He has forgiven us.

However, forgiving (or releasing) carries powerful implications for both sides:

Our sin will not be used against us anymore. It cannot be used as a bartering chip for retribution or a tool for inflicting further shame.

Our sin will not be talked about to others. The person forgiving commits not to gossip about it to others or share it unnecessarily in order to slander reputations.

Our sin will not be dwelt on anymore. The person we sinned against will not hover over our sins or make a habit of thinking about them. While we're not capable of forgetting entirely, the forgiver commits not to focus on our failures anymore.

All of these are true when God forgives us. Our sin is as far as the East is from the West (Psalm 103:12); He doesn't speak of our failures to others, and He is concentrating on His righteousness in Christ, not our wretchedness.

True forgiveness from God brings release. This release comes after we confess our sins to God, and in His grace and loving kindness, He forgives us through Christ. We are promised: "If we confess our sin, God is faithful and just to forgive" (1 John 1:9).

CONFESSION IS KEY

One of the greatest fears people live with is the fear of being found out. We are a people of many secrets. We have thoughts we would never want to be published, actions we never want to be mentioned, and motives that would mortify us if they were exposed. Hidden sin produces anxiety. Like trying to keep a balloon underwater, our unconfessed sins will cause us great angst that will someday pop up in ways we never wanted it to—with God or others. We can keep looking over our shoulders in hopes that we will not be found out, or we can come clean before God and those we've hurt.

We confess our sins by calling them what they are. The air in the balloon is released when we finally acknowledge we messed up and failed God's expectations. God calls us to confess our sins as a prerequisite for being forgiven. I believe this divine order allows us to feel the weight of release, for humility to be real, and for God's forgiveness to be recognized.

There was a season in my life where I had to give repeated tours of "my hall of shame." My wife was by my side through it all and had to hear the tour over and over again. Confession of my sin always started with, "What I did was sinful and wrong in the eyes of the Lord." Every time I had to utter those words, as painful as they were, I was calling sin what it was.

James 5:16 says, "Therefore, confess your sins to one another and pray for one another, that you may be healed. The prayer of a righteous person has great power as it is working." Telling God and others—specifically those I sinned against—where I went off course and transgressed was the beginning of healing. Whether it's at our moment of salvation or in our daily relationship with Christ, God looks for us to confess our sins, and then He imparts forgiveness to us.

In the same way, when we forgive others, we *release* them from the debt owed us for the hurt they caused after they have confessed their wrongdoing. Christ-followers are commanded to forgive others in the same way God forgave us.

APOLOGIZING AND ASKING FOR FORGIVENESS ARE DIFFERENT

As Christians, when we sin against God or someone else, we must go back and confess our sins and ask for forgiveness. It is true for any blatant, flagrant, ongoing sin that is damaging to Christ and others. Blatant sin includes the times where we violate the commands of God by lying, cheating, stealing, manipulating, slandering, and intentionally hurting someone for selfish gain.

When we know we violated the commands of God, we will feel a level of conviction that can portray itself as anxiety. Our hearts are stirred and unsettled when we do something wrong. Like a flashing alarm on life's dashboard, we are being told to go back and ask for forgiveness.

However, this does not mean that we go around begging for forgiveness for every little thing we do wrong. That would be a full-time job. Rather, we are diligent to confess our blatant sins before God and those we hurt and ask for their forgiveness.

Asking for forgiveness and apologizing are different. We apologize—saying, "I am sorry"—for the *oops* moments in life. To say I am sorry is to express sorrow over something incidental and accidental. For example, when I bump into someone else by accident, I apologize for my mistake, but I don't have an all-out repentance session right there in the parking lot. With all genuineness, we should express our sorrow over our mistakes.

While sin is the ultimate "mistaking" of God's desire for us, sin is not just covered with an "I'm sorry." Sin is not just a mistake; it is wrong and hurtful to God and others. Nor should the person we hurt excuse it by saying, "It's not a big deal ..." or "That's water under the bridge ..." Rather, when we blatantly sin, we confess by calling it out. The person we're confessing our sin to then should announce forgiveness by saying, "I forgive you for _____."

Nowhere in the Bible does it say to apologize for sin. We are told to confess sin and ask for forgiveness.

Christians who make light of sin end up forfeiting the power of forgiveness.

Anxiety can come from instances of sin and character issues. Both types of sin must be confessed and sought forgiveness for from God and the offended party. Not all sin has to be confessed to all people; the circle of knowledge can match the size of the circle of offense and repentance in most cases. Yet when we tell others where we went wrong, release can come, allowing for a decrease in anxiety and an embrace of Christ's forgiveness.

GO AHEAD, THROW

I sat in front of my staff once and told them about something I had done wrong. Nearly all of them met me with an incredible sense of grace, understanding, and forgiveness. There is this older (and wiser) gentleman, Eston, on our facility staff who has weathered many storms in life. I will never forget his response after I shared my failure in that room full of staff and elders. He was the first to speak. "Well, who am I to throw the first stone?"

That day, through tears and empathy, the staff met me with a practice of forgiveness that revealed the character of Christ. In John 8, the religious leaders of the day brought a woman before Jesus. This woman was accused of being a prostitute—someone deserving of death by stoning, according to the Jewish Law. Jesus told those who were without sin to throw the first stone. Rocks fell with repeated thuds as they dropped their stones and walked away—the oldest and most mature leaving first.

When we are mature in Christ, we will be quick to drop our rocks of unforgiveness. It is those who are less mature or do not understand the Gospel of Christ who will be quick to judge and throw verbal stones of slander and gossip. If this happens to you, as it has to me, it will produce tremendous anxiety. However, those who falsely accuse us or hold our sins over us are not bigger or more powerful than the Savior who has forgiven us.

"I forgive you" are three of the strongest words we can ever hear another person say, second only to the words "I love you." I know what it's like to long for both of these phrases to ring in my ears. We all fail and desire to know that we are forgiven and loved in spite of our failures.

We may intellectually know we are forgiven and loved, but what does it mean to *live like it?*

WHAT IF I CAN'T FORGIVE MYSELF?

I am familiar with the self-condemning messages my heart and the enemy preach to me daily. Not a day goes by where my hope does not wither under the weight of my shame. I have to preach the powerful Gospel message to myself every day to drown out the lies of other people in my life who believe I will never be fully forgiven.

Paul knew our hope would be tested every day; this is why he speaks of regularly renewing it in 2 Corinthians 4:1–6. He writes, "Do not lose heart!" This insinuates that *we can* lose heart. But by the truth of the Gospel and the power of the Holy Spirit, we must press on.

I have had many people seek counseling in my office who tell me they cannot forgive themselves. I know the feeling. Then I ask them, "Has God forgiven you?" The reply so far has been 100 percent "Yes!" Then I say to them, "If God has forgiven you, then who are you to withhold forgiveness as if you have more power than God? His forgiveness demands that you let go of your shame and start living like a forgiven person."

REPENTANCE IS THE FIRST STEP TO LIVING FORGIVEN

Repentance is when the Holy Spirit enables a supernatural change of our motives, thinking, and behaviors. When we're made new in Christ, it changes us on the deepest level: our motives (Ephesians 4:22–24). Following Christ is not merely some moralistic therapeutic deism; rather, following Him changes us from the inside out, not the outside in.

We do not start with some *far-off* idea that God demands behavior change, and we hope that change eventually affects our hearts or brings us inner peace. Being changed starts with the message of Jesus's *indwelling* our hearts with the power of the Holy Spirit, who changes our motives. It results in a change of thinking and behavior.

There is a progression of *repentance* that leads to *the fruit of repentance*. If a person is forgiven, following their confession of sin, then they have repented of their sin by committing to God and others that they will no longer carry on as they once did. Verbal confession is the proof of genuine, godly sorrow evidenced in a sustained and changed motive, thought, and action.

A repentant and forgiven person will strive for righteousness instead of walking in the way of the wicked (Psalm 1:1–4). This evidence of repentance and forgiveness should show itself in confident living in Christ. The benefits that come from knowing you are forgiven in Christ need to manifest in your life in six profound ways:

1. Your prayer life is vital to your everyday survival. You may have prayed in the past, but when you understand you're forgiven, your prayer life doesn't simply return to what it was before. Now you better understand to Whom you are praying. A forgiven person internalizes the mercy they receive in such a way that when they pray, they know they don't deserve to be heard. We count it all the more a privilege to be able to approach the throne of grace and do so often in prayer (Hebrews 4:16).

2. You long for God's Word like never before. As I walk in the forgiveness of God, I can't get enough of God's Word. The time I get in the Bible is sweeter when I understand my dependence on it. As it relates to God's mercy over my mistakes, the Psalms seem to have the perfect words to help bring healing and fuller confidence in Christ. The duty of reading God's Word as a daily discipline becomes an anticipated delight in my routine.

3. Your confidence is not found in yourself. As a follower of Jesus Christ, my identity is no longer in myself. I am made new in Christ and derive my confidence from His work in my life (Jeremiah 17:7). When people criticize me or talk about what a horrible sinner I am, my posture is to agree with them, not defend. I will be the first in line to build a case against myself; I am the worst sinner I know because I know my sin the most. For that reason, I resolved that finding confidence solely in me is a useless waste of time. I will always fail myself and others, *but Christ will never fail me.*

4. Your actions are humble and caring toward others. A forgiven person is kind, tenderhearted, and forgiving toward others because they understand they are forgiven first by Christ Jesus (Ephesians 4:32). If a person is harsh, hard-hearted, and lacking empathy or care as a fellow sinner, then they may not understand the magnitude of forgiveness Christ offers. In fact, they may not be saved.

If a person does not accept his weaknesses and Christ's forgiveness for them, he will not be able or quick to give this kind of forgiveness to others. He will be critical, quick to accuse (Matthew 7:3), and judgmental. Avoid such people and avoid being such a person (2 Timothy 3:5).

5. You find freedom in what is true in Christ—not in *what could be true* in your circumstances. Our circumstances tell us the daily story that life is brutal and out of control. Tim Keller said, "When pain and suffering come upon us, we finally see not only that we are not in control of our lives but that we never were."[4] If we are trying to find peace from the right setting or surrounding, we may find it for a moment—like in a beach chair in Fiji—but that won't last for a lifetime.

Our freedom and joy are not found in the circumstances; they are found only in Christ (Philippians 4:5–7). If you're dealing with feelings of anxiety or depression over your past mistakes, perhaps you have not fully accepted the grace of Christ in your life. Live like a forgiven person and stop trying to give yourself peace by controlling circumstances.

6. You walk with your chin up and with a smile. The countenance of a forgiven person is bright. A forgiven and glad person will show it on his face. Proverbs 15:13 says, "A glad heart makes a cheerful face." A forgiven person will smile, laugh, and show he has accepted the forgiveness of Christ. It is not trite; it is the result of genuine forgiveness. Will he still have critics who hate when he smiles, laughs, and goes on with life? Yes, he will; that's certainly the case in my life. However, those critics don't control the forgiveness of Christ, nor should they control my countenance over what Christ has given me.

"AS"

When it comes to letting go of the pain others have caused us, we forgive them as Christ forgave us. Without a good theology of forgiveness in our lives, we can easily grow bitter, angry, and resentful. Jesus told us to forgive someone who repents of his sin—and if he keeps on repenting, we keep on forgiving (Luke 17:3–4), just *as* Jesus does with us.

The word "as" is important when understanding how to forgive. Ephesians 4:32 says, "Be kind to one another, tenderhearted, forgiving one another, *as* God in Christ forgave you" (emphasis mine). Jesus taught His disciples—and us—to pray "and forgive us our debts, *as* we also have forgiven our debtors" (Matthew 6:12, emphasis mine). The "*as*" indicates "in the same way." The way we forgive others is the same way God forgives us.

As we confess our sin, He is faithful and just to forgive us. *As* those who sinned against us, we also are faithful to forgive. We realize how much we have been forgiven, so we are willing to forgive much.

Forgiveness is hard, but thank God that it's not impossible. Christ made the way for us to be forgiven, and He enables us to forgive others.

THREE STEPS TOWARD THE END OF ANXIETY

ACT

Seek forgiveness from someone you sinned against by confessing your sin to them and asking forgiveness. Also, identify where you have chosen to stay in unforgiveness and bitterness and ask God to help you forgive.

READ

Unpacking Forgiveness by Chris Brauns will help you to better understand biblical forgiveness and find answers to many related misconceptions.

MEMORIZE

Commit to memory Ephesians 4:32, remembering you have been forgiven much so you can forgive much.

CHAPTER 14

ABANDON THE SELF-HELP GOSPEL

START WITH SCRIPTURE
Ephesians 1:13–14; 1 John 5

CORE PRINCIPLE FOURTEEN

The antidote to anxiety is not sourced from our hearts. It can only come from the perfect peace found in Jesus, our Savior. No amount of "bootstrapping," self-help, or "I'll fix it myself" can compare to the peace of God that our hearts can barely comprehend.

When I was fifteen years old, I set out on a day hike in the woods with my friend Eric. It was summertime, and we didn't have a care in the world. We were both high schoolers and felt invincible. We had been part of a Boy Scout troop with both of our dads serving as leaders, so we probably had a false sense of security from all the parental guidance and protection. We thought we had this camping and hiking thing nailed. We packed up for the day and set out on an epic adventure. We planned our route, packed our snacks, and prepared our map.

When I say we prepared our map, I mean we calculated the bearings to and from each major landmark. We felt secure in our preparations. So when it came time to hit the trail, we ensured we had everything and even asked one small but significant question: "Do we have the map?"

We mutually decided, "Why do we need a map?" We thought a compass and the calculated bearings we scribbled on a paper would suffice. As long as we had our bearings, we didn't need a map, right? With far too much confidence in our abilities, we decided to leave the map behind.

Here is a bit of free advice: If you're going on a hike led by a map and compass, both the compass and the map are essential. Without the map, the compass is nothing but a dangling necklace of uselessness.

GETTING LOST IN THE FOREST OF ANXIETY

Yes, we had a great time! It was one of the most enjoyable days in the woods I've ever had—that is, until the sun started setting. It was as if it never dawned on us—until it was too late—that we did need the map.

Without our map, we had to hit the landmarks dead on. If we didn't—which we didn't—then it would be nearly impossible to find our way out with only a compass.

But hey, an A-plus for effort. We tried it the hard way. With everything in us, we tried to use only the compass to get us back to the trailhead. As the evening grew darker, the trailhead became the least of our concern. Soon we were just looking for any signs of human life.

If you've ever been lost, even slightly, then you will identify with this statement: you don't care where you are at the moment; you want to be sure someone else knows you're missing.

It wasn't long before we came upon a road. A road! This was a good sign. The sun had set completely, and the only decision before us was to take a left or a right. We looked at our compasses, as if that would help, and took a left. We walked for what felt like hours when suddenly two headlights peeked over the hill. It was Eric's dad driving down the road as part of the newly assembled search party.

We were excited to be rescued, but we didn't sense the same excitement from Eric's dad.

We knew from his stony expression that we might be getting a well-deserved lecture when we got home. In a low, monotone voice, he said, "Get in the car. We've sent out everyone looking for you."

It was a long, hushed ride back to the trailhead, but I do remember Eric's dad getting on the search radio channel and saying, "I've got the packages." Though he had dehumanized us from people to packages, we didn't care. We were glad to be found.

I don't remember the full debrief (lecture) we received from our dads, but I do remember it included the stern admonition always to take a map. The reproach came with the words: "You can only find your way out of the forest by trusting your tools." That has stuck with me to this day.

This same principle can be applied to our lives in panic, fear, worry, and stress. *You can only find the way out of the dark forest of anxiety if you trust your tools.*

The two greatest tools God ever gave us for finding our way back home are the Bible and prayer. The Bible remains forever a reliable source of direction—the map showing God's pathway for us to follow. The Holy Spirit has been for all of eternity; He is part of "true north," God Himself—our compass.

God's Word is a map of sorts, but without the guidance of the Holy Spirit, the map isn't going to make much sense. The Holy Spirit, serving as the compass, comes along and enlightens us as to how we are to live and where we are to go. Both are necessary and complement each other. Of course, there are times I still get lost in the woods of anxiety, but I've found that it is because I've chosen to neglect one of the vital tools God has already given me.

When I underutilize the Bible or ignore the promptings of the Holy Spirit, I'm just "bushwhacking" my way through life. God's tools help us know His promises and principles, even when we don't feel His presence.

Maybe you've asked questions like:

Where is this path leading?

Why is God not making the right choice clearer?

If God loves me, then why isn't He directing me?

If God is in control, why is everything such a mess?

These are questions we've all asked in different ways at various times. When God's presence is not prevalent, neither is peace. As we found in Chapter 6, God promises He will give you peace—even if the path you have to walk is difficult.

Do you believe Him? God has a very long and extensive track record of never, ever breaking a promise.

A PROMISE KEPT OVER THREE THOUSAND YEARS (AND COUNTING)

Some eight hundred years before Christ's birth, the Holy Spirit inspired the prophet Isaiah to pen a hymn of praise. He was speaking about a promised Messiah who was to come. We now know that God gave clear promises with a setup for specific fulfillment. God never forgets to do anything He says He will do—including the promise found in Isaiah 26:3: "You keep him in perfect peace whose mind is stayed on You, because he trusts in You."

Those first two words are powerful: "You keep." Translated, they mean, "You guard as with a fort." When we are at our wits' end, we need nothing more than the fortress of our God to surround us with Himself. God sustains us in the stronghold of His Son (John 6:37–42), and the result for us is perfect peace.

Where does He keep us, according to this passage? "In perfect peace." In Hebrew, this is simply the same word used twice. It would read "peace peace" or "peace in peace." He keeps us in doubled-down peace, reiterating the same word to make clear its potency and perfection. It is a perfect, lasting, withstanding, steadfast, and faultless kind of peace. This peace may look like:

- Your life is falling apart, but you remain calm—not apathetic or unaffected, but calm
- You're experiencing inconceivable circumstances that leave everyone else confused. Friends might say, "How is all this happening to you at once?" Yet, you are assured in faith and are persevering through calamity
- Despite overwhelming circumstances, you are not frantic or panicked but confident and serene
- You are intentional about praying, pausing, and processing circumstances as they unfold in your life

A person with perfect peace is not worried about what this life will bring. Focus on these words from Psalm 112:7: "He is not afraid of bad news; his heart is firm, trusting in the LORD." Perfect peace of God is a result of trust in God. Even bad news seems like no news when our trust and hope are in a sovereign God. We have to believe that He is allowing all things to happen for a purpose.

My mentor, Randy Patten, will ask me often, "Why would a sovereign God allow this to happen?" I've grown to expect this question after I recount to him something hard or seemingly out of control in my life. Even though I know the question is coming, I never get tired of discovering the answer with Randy's help. He always points me back to the fact that a person who trusts that God is sovereign will be able to wring all the good out of every situation.

Pointing us back to trusting God is more than any other superficial answer or crutch in our lives.

The kind of peace that surpasses understanding—which doesn't make sense, considering reality—can only come from trusting God's sovereignty. Any time peace is used in the Old Testament, it is associated with the presence of God. Later in the New Testament, we see that the peace of God comes through Jesus Christ. It is as if both of the Testaments are emphasizing that there is no real peace outside of God. Philippians 4:7 reminds us, "And the peace of God, which surpasses all understanding, will guard your hearts and your minds in Christ Jesus." While we may have acute turmoil and strife around us, we will experience perfect peace—but *only if* we trust God.

LORD JEHOVAH IS THE LORD UNCHANGING

I recently heard a quote that grabbed my heart. I was with my brother on a Wednesday night, and we talked about the trials of life. Sitting surrounded by my kids covered in ice cream, my brother quoted a popular statement that is often attributed to Charles Spurgeon: "I have learned to kiss the wave that throws me against the Rock of Ages."[1] Only a person who understands the value of the Rock of Ages can kiss the waves of trials and tribulations.

With lumps in our throats and tears brimming on our eyelids, we say, "Bring it on, world! My hope rests in the unchanging, steady hand of God." We can learn to kiss the wave because Christ is near to us and supreme over all things.

Isaiah provided this valuable insight:

> The path of the righteous is level;
> You make level the way of the righteous.
> In the path of Your judgments,
> O LORD, we wait for You;

Your name and remembrance
are the desire of our soul (Isaiah 26:7–8).

Our perfect peace is made full, and our paths smoothed and straightened, by living right with God. The righteous person is the one who lives right before God. In all public and private matters, in good times and bad, the righteous person longs to be at peace with God, obedient to His will.

God is the One who "makes level" the paths of the righteous person. We don't have to worry about steep climbs, insurmountable peaks, and death valleys when we walk with God. It doesn't mean that trials will be removed or that our journey through life will be a stroll in the park. God does say that one of the main blessings of the righteous is that God "makes their way straight before their face" (Psalm 4:8). Also, He "leads them in a plain path" (Psalm 27:11) and "shows them the way they are to walk in" (Psalm 143:8), so they are free from doubt and perplexity.[2]

The path may still be rough, but as we walk on, trusting God, it is as if there is no climb too hard or too steep. This kind of peace makes the pursuit of righteousness worth it. No momentary pleasure can win over the promise of perfect peace.

I lived in Chicago through much of my twenties. For one year, I rented a room in the basement of a couple's home. It was a time when I was being smashed by the waves of grief and loneliness. There were nights when I would cry so hard in their basement; I would go in the shower and let the water run to cover the sound of my crying.

My soul was in anguish, but when I yearned for God, perfect peace eventually came. My spirit needed direction. My mind had to win over my heart with what I knew to be true rather than what I wanted to feel. This kind of peace comes from an intentional pursuit of obedience and righteousness—not fickle sinfulness or the small impact of self-help.

ABANDON THE SELF-HELP GOSPEL

Self-sufficiency is an idol of choice today. There is a baseline cultural narrative that says leaning on yourself and making something of yourself is the only way to live. We make plans, and we make those plans happen. Culture seems to tell us we're weak if we rely on anyone else. As the U.S. Army's motto states: "Be an Army of One."

While Christianity believes in working hard and doing your share, Christianity stands opposed to presumption and self-reliance. Conversely, trusting in yourself is opposed to Christianity. We trust Christ, not ourselves, for our daily spiritual guidance. So are we weak? No!

The Gospel of Jesus Christ teaches that our strength is found when we trust God more. He is worth trusting, and ultimately, our lives are in His hands. Making plans without considering God is antithetical to the core of Christianity; we are called to trust Jesus, not ourselves.

When Jesus spoke to His followers in John 16, He was not merely giving them knowledge of what the Father would and could do for them. Jesus was moving His followers to total trust with a longer memory of the goodness and sovereignty of God. While this passage is directly speaking about persecution, there is an application for any hardship we face.

Before giving His disciples the promise of peace, Jesus told them that trouble *would* come. We will experience persecution and pain inflicted by evil people and the evil one, Satan. He did not say it "may" come. Not "it could happen every few years depending on how faithful you are ..." Jesus's words are adamant: we *will* experience trouble in this world *because* we are followers of Jesus.

It can seem like an odd way to comfort someone, but Jesus did it to remind them—and us—of God's sovereignty. For us to experience the peace of God, we must have genuine humility and utter desperation for Him amid our overwhelming emotions.

Jesus's words ring throughout the centuries into our hearts: "Take heart; I have overcome the world." Only God has overcome the world (John 16:31–33). What a powerful and promising statement! Nothing else has overcome the world; therefore, nothing will overcome you! The only reason we can have peace is that God is in control.

The world will tell you to overcome challenges in your strength and try to control your circumstances and emotions in your power or by your own devices. **This is not the message of the Gospel of Jesus Christ. The self-help gospel is a perversion drawn from the pride and sin of humankind.** The only way we can overcome is by the power of God through Christ in our lives. The Gospel demonstrates that we have a problem—we are infected with sin and separated from our holy God. But God, in His rich mercy, gave us His Son's resurrection from the dead to prove that He has overcome the world, including our most downcast emotions.

The conquering Jesus, described in John 16:33, is both for today and the future. Today, as believers, we can overcome sin, temptation, and despair through Christ, knowing that one day we will overcome Satan and the kingdom of darkness through Christ's final victory.

Why should we yearn for the true Gospel of Jesus Christ? I'd like to humbly suggest that all of us yearn for Christ because:

God gives us peace by giving us purpose. He gives peace to those "whose mind is stayed on You" (Isaiah 26:3) and provision as we travel the road of life.

God gives us relationships with others who provide wisdom to make decisions.

God gives us encouragement by His nearness, saying, "Don't despair, stay on the path I have marked out for you. Keep your eyes on Me!" (See Hebrews 12:1–4.)

Perfect peace begins by understanding that your mind, heart, and motivations must be grounded in righteous living before our

Almighty God. There are three key components that will ensure your heart is guided by peace—not anxiety, fear, or despair:

Keep your mind fixed on Christ. A mind fixed on God's glory sees life through His eyes. You trust Him to be in control of the outcomes, and beyond all human reason, you seek Him for clarity, confidence, and direction.

Direct your desires to Christ. Trust our unchanging Creator for security and provision. When you begin to love or desire anything more than Him, check your heart and diligently reprioritize Him above all worldly things.

Choose to live for Christ. It is your decision to live out your everyday opportunities for God's pleasure alone. In other words, make up your mind "to walk in a manner worthy of the Lord" (Colossians 1:10). Rid yourself of the things in your life that need to go to make more room for what God wants to do in and through you.

In the trials of life, suddenly, the things of this world become of little importance. Why? Because you realize what Solomon finally discovered: "Everything is meaningless...life is a vapor" (see Ecclesiastes 1; James 4:13–17). In the same way, when we are seeking God, we let go of the things we value and let loose our souls to value Christ above all things. A heart held in perfect peace whispers, "His voice may be silent, but His presence is all I need."

The waves of life will crash against us, but they are not seen as evil when we understand they are pushing us onto the Rock of Ages, the Rock of our salvation, our Savior Jesus Christ.

It is between the waves and the Rock that we find our perfect peace. That is where our Savior feels the closest to our hearts.

THREE STEPS TOWARD THE END OF ANXIETY

CONNECT

Ask a friend to pray with you and help you see God's goodness through the Gospel of Jesus Christ in your life.

REFLECT

Take a prayer walk and thank God for what the Gospel reveals to you about His nature and character. List these attributes out and be specific. For example, "God, you are merciful because…" or "God, your power is real to me because…"

READ

Study Romans 1–4 and keep track of four essential elements, marking them or highlighting with different colors: God's role, sin's role, Christ's role, and our necessary response. Be reminded of the true power of God through Christ that will save you.

CHAPTER 15

BE FAZED BY NOTHING

CORE PRINCIPLE FIFTEEN

I don't have to be anxious about being anxious ever again.
Tomorrow has enough worries of its own, so I will focus on being
bold and courageous today with the presence of Christ in my life.

M *oses is dead. Joshua is in charge now.*
This Old Testament story is told so matter-of-factly in
Joshua 1 that I can feel the adrenaline racing through Joshua's veins
as he assumed command of the nation of Israel. Moses—Joshua's
hero, mentor, and father figure, not to mention the one with direct
access to God—was dead, and now Joshua needed to fill Moses's
role. Let's pick up the story from Joshua 1:1–3:

> After the death of Moses the servant of the LORD, the
> LORD said to Joshua the son of Nun, Moses' assistant,
> "Moses My servant is dead. Now therefore arise, go over
> this Jordan, you and all this people, into the land that I

am giving to them, to the people of Israel. Every place that the sole of your foot will tread upon I have given to you, just as I promised to Moses."

It would've been easy for Joshua and others to believe God's plan stopped when Moses died. But that would be short-sighted. God had already told them the plan; He made a promise to bring Israel into the land of Canaan, and as we've already learned, God never breaks His promises. Just because Moses was dead didn't mean God was finished. God's story *never* ends simply because someone else's does, but it's easy to think that way. Our memory can be suspect in the face of grief. The promises of God can quickly fade in our memories when we face death—death of our dreams, death of opportunities, death of responsibilities, and especially the death of others.

Though Joshua probably wanted to quit or at least mourn Moses for a while, that wasn't God's idea. Joshua knew God's plan was still moving forward—that's what Joshua saw while serving Moses for many years. He watched Moses meet with God at the Tent of Meeting (Exodus 33:11). Joshua even traveled partway up the holy mountain of Sinai with Moses (Exodus 24:13; 32:17). Out of all the nation of Israel, Joshua had the most reason to trust God now that Moses was gone.

Moses was called "Servant of the Lord" (Joshua 1, 13, 24:29; Judges 2:8). It had to be unnerving and anxiety-fueling for Joshua.

When God said, "My servant Moses is dead, now you..." Joshua probably wondered, "But I'm not Moses..." and maybe God replied, "Correct...but I'm still God."

Many times, we forget that God is God—unchanging, always working, always fulfilling promises, and always empowering. He is in the business of accomplishing His will for His glory through broken people like Joshua...like you...and like me.

RESIGNING OUR HEARTS TO OBEDIENCE

Did Joshua argue with God? Did he have any other choice but obedience? Maybe Joshua wondered where he could send his resignation letter. Actually, I don't think he was like that at all. I imagine he was terrified and humbled before God in a way that evoked only obedience. When we right-size our perspective of God, He has a supernatural ability to shrink our fears in proportion to our newfound perspective of faith. The promises and presence of God will always diminish the fears and emotions we face or imagine.

The "patriarchal promise," first uttered to Abraham (Genesis 12:1–3) involved three key elements: *legacy*—Abraham's descendants would become a great nation; *blessing*—they would enjoy the blessings of living in covenant relationship with Yahweh—and were in turn to be a blessing to the nations; and *land*—the Promised Land of Israel (Genesis 12:1, 5–7; 15:18).

The first two had come to pass by the end of the Pentateuch—the first five books of the Old Testament. However, the third part of the promise—land—was not realized yet for a good reason. Abraham's descendants still lived on the plains of Moab, east of the Jordan River, outside the Land of Promise (Numbers 22:1; Deuteronomy 34:8). Their ancestors had grumbled and doubted God, so He made them dwell in the wilderness until they died off. The next generation was the one who would see God's promises come to fruition. The dominant theme of the book of Joshua is the Lord's faithfulness in fulfilling all His "good promises." Joshua 21:45 records this: "Not one word of all the good promises that the Lord had made to the house of Israel had failed; all came to pass."

So when God promised Joshua (1:3) that "I will give you every place...." Joshua could rest assured that God always keeps His promises. If God said He'd give the land to Israel, God would fulfill His promise. This is applicable for fighting reoccurring anxiety. Track with me.

I AM WITH YOU

God asked Joshua to do some daunting things:

Take over because Moses is dead. When you've seen God's chosen fulfill their callings, and now you're God's chosen, that can be a terrifying responsibility to fulfill.

Lead My people across the Jordan. No small task. The Jordan River was in a valley ten miles across. The Jordan pumps six million tons of water into the Dead Sea every day. It was like marching two million people across Class Five rapids!

Conquer the land I've promised you. It meant battle after battle—just read the first twelve chapters of Joshua.

Divide the land accordingly. It certainly came with its fair share of mediation and turf wars between the Israelites (explained in Joshua 13–21).

God made a personal promise to Joshua in Joshua 1:5: "No man shall be able to stand before you all the days of your life. Just as I was with Moses, so I will be with you. I will not leave you or forsake you."

God promised the Israelites the land. He promised them His presence. However, the promises of God did not negate their responsibility to step out in faith and take what was given (compare verses 9 and 18). The same is true for you—you have to move forward in faith to embrace your eternal calling and the promises of Christ, no matter your fears or worries.

Yes, there are going to be tasks God will ask you to do even when you're a nervous, anxious mess. You need the courage at that moment to press on and fulfill God's calling on your life. Just like Moses, and just like Joshua, you don't have to do this life alone. God is with you!

It's easy to forget this promise from God. There is no more practical promise God can give us than the promise of His presence.

We forget just how close He is—what He sees, what He provides—and because we forget, we then forfeit our true source of strength. Joshua certainly knew God was always with Moses. There had to be those nights around the campfire when Moses recounted for Joshua how he encountered the burning bush and heard God's reassurance to him: "I will be with you..." (Exodus 3:12). God kept that promise to Moses, and Joshua was able to experience it firsthand.

God's promise to be with Joshua allowed Him to command him then to "be strong and courageous" (verse 9). God is not going to require something of us that He is not willing to provide for us. God was giving Joshua His presence, and therefore, God could ignite Joshua's faith.

Joshua couldn't just sit in mourning. He had to be strong and courageous to do what God asked him to do, whether he felt like it or not. Human responsibility and divine sovereignty are meant to walk hand in hand. Of course, God will do His work as only He can, but God requires us to have faith in the process. Every miracle Christ performed asked for faith from the person or people He was healing.

GOD'S PEOPLE LIVE ON PROMISES, NOT EXPLANATIONS

Analytical, detailed, type-A personalities like me may want a full explanation of what it means to have God's presence in our lives. As frustrating and anxiety-inducing as it is, though, we need to acknowledge there are moments when we need to believe God because we don't have the luxury of fully understanding the moment. Even the best Christian philosopher in the world cannot explain to us how an infinite God involves Himself in the finite details of our lives. And yet, God does.

"Am I a God who is near," declares the LORD, "and not a God far off? Can a man hide himself in hiding places so I do not see him?" declares the LORD. "Do I not fill the heavens and the earth?" declares the LORD (Jeremiah 23:23–24).

You can either choose to be confounded that God is everywhere or comforted by this truth. He knows your lies and insecurities. He knows your hiding spots and shame sources. He knows your facades. He knows your search history. He knows your guilty pleasures, and all the while, He loves you just the same.

I choose to be comforted by the fact that God is close to the brokenhearted (Psalm 34:18) and uses my weaknesses and sinfulness to remind me of my desperate need for Him.

In the end, our pain and weakness are tools in God's toolbox for sanctification—His constant work to perfect Christ's image in us. We need to recognize, like Paul, that when God allows hard circumstances in our lives, He will still glorify Himself in the end (2 Corinthians 1:7). By trusting God's goodness and power in our struggles, we are made more into the likeness of His Son (Philippians 3:10).

God is in control of the endgame, and He will not allow His followers to go through *anything* that does not glorify Him. God can be glorified through us—even in death. In spite of the sinful fall of man, He gives us a second chance for a divine relationship with Him through Jesus Christ. It is in that relationship where I find eternal hope, no matter what may happen next!

Yes, we will suffer, and yes, God is still good and sovereign. Both truths can simultaneously exist, and this calls us to be strong and courageous as we trust Him.

Having courage is believing what you cannot see while trusting God for the outcome. Faith is simply courage clinging to Christ for dear life. We cannot walk around like the Cowardly Lion from *The Wizard of Oz*. God calls us to mighty works and loves to use us in great ways, but so many of us are walking about in fear, not knowing if our lives reflect His calling.

True strength—a strength that's authentic, lasting, unchanging—and courage come solely from Christ's presence in our lives. We live with our back against the cross and with His Word as our sword in hand. Jesus spoke a similar promise to the one in Joshua after giving the Great Commission in Matthew 28: "I am with you always, even to the end of the age."

You may think this promise is not for you and that it was only for people in the Bible. You may be struggling to take this promise from *believing* that God is with you to *knowing* God is with you. If Joshua only went on what he knew and chose not to live in faith, he never would have had the strength and courage to do great things for God.

Joshua didn't have a PowerPoint, spreadsheet, roadmap, or diagram to show him what would happen next. His emotions may have been raging, but his faith was fixed on God. Our strength and courage come when we live on God's promises, not His explanations.

HOLD ON

I recently visited my child's Christian elementary school on a Friday. I had a full day before me and was struggling to take the time to stay for the all-school chapel. However, my son asked me to stay to watch his class lead a worship song, so I stayed. I sat in the back row, ready to make a quick exit. I didn't expect to be impacted. I was just going to catch a bit of video on my phone, give the good-ol' dad wink, whisper, "Good job, buddy," and then leave.

But God had me there to hear their little voices sing a truth that cut me right to the heart.

As the chapel progressed, it came time to sing a hymn; this was a regular Friday occurrence. They put the words to a one-hundred-year-old song on the screen, and a few hundred elementary kids started singing these words (read them slowly):

> *When I fear my faith will fail*
> *Christ will hold me fast*
> *When the tempter would prevail*
> *He will hold me fast*
> *I could never keep my hold*
> *Through life's fearful path*
> *For my love is often cold*
> *He must hold me fast.*
> *He will hold me fast*
> *He will hold me fast*
> *For my Savior loves me so*
> *He will hold me fast*

The song goes on, but I couldn't. My stomach was in my throat, and the refreshing words of God's promise to hold on caused my tears to release. It was one of those moments where I just hoped my son's friends wouldn't say, "Chandler, look at your dad crying in the back row..." but I couldn't help it.

It is clear to me, as I hold on to God, that He is holding on to me even more.

Jude 1:24 says, "To Him who is able to keep you...." He holds on to us, preserving us, using us, and comforting us. He keeps us in perfect peace as long as our eyes remain fixed on Him (Isaiah 26:3).

The greatest promise God can give is Himself. He did that through Christ. The only way to have true strength and courage is to have Christ's presence in your life. Anything else will fail you, but Christ never will. As Romans 8:31 reminds our hearts, "If God is with us, who can be against us?"

Imagine if we lived truly tapped into the strength and courage of Christ. We could face our trials with stamina, our adversaries with boldness, our callings with confidence, and our Lord with humility.

The chief end of your anxiety may be for God to do something in and through you that you can't even fathom. It was true for Joshua. So be strong and courageous, my friend. God is with you. There is nothing to fear with Christ on our side.

THREE STEPS TOWARD THE END OF ANXIETY

ACT
List your objections toward God's call to action in your life and humbly ask Him to change your perspective.

REFLECT
Does your anxiety come from a deep desire to get what you want or to not lose what you already have? Does it consume you? Do you obsess about it? Do you sin to get it or keep it? Ask God to help put your desire in its rightful place. Better yet, ask God to help you ensure He has His rightful place in your life as Lord and supreme over all other desires.

MEMORIZE
Commit Hebrews 4:15–16 to memory. Write down how your confidence can be strengthened by knowing that Christ empathizes with your weaknesses.

CHAPTER 16

WELCOME TO THE STRONGER YOU

START WITH SCRIPTURE
John 15:1–5; Isaiah 40

CORE PRINCIPLE SIXTEEN
Waiting upon the Lord means that I bind myself to Him and His purposes. It can give me the ultimate confidence and strength that can only come from His ever-present Spirit.

With rain pouring down in buckets, I drove my 1978 baby-poop-gold Chevrolet Suburban back to town after speaking at a conference. I had all my gear in the back—poles for my ministry booth, banners, books, handouts, and all sorts of other paraphernalia. On the passenger seat beside me sat a bag of half-eaten Fire Cheetos, and a huge Mountain Dew in the cup holder kept me awake.

As I drove, the old windshield wipers did little to improve visibility, and the heavy rain made it extremely hard to see. No "small" storm could stop me, though. I was on a mission to get home.

I soon found myself behind a huge eighteen-wheeler that was splashing water, making things much worse. I decided to give the ol' Suburban all it had and punched the accelerator to get around the semi. Two-thirds of the way past the truck, I started hydroplaning, swerving like a water skier on the wet roads. I lost control and became a ping-pong ball between the truck and the five-foot concrete median to the left of me.

At that point, everything went into slow motion. The Mountain Dew flew across the windshield, the windows shattered, and the poles from the back of the vehicle hurtled forward like a battering ram, right into my shoulders.

What probably lasted only a tenth of a second felt like ten minutes. I couldn't gain control of the Suburban, no matter how hard I tried, and I was at the mercy of whatever would hit me next.

By the grace of God, there was a twelve-foot rut carved in the concrete that caught my left tires, popping them and catching the rims, stopping the car abruptly. The semi kept on rolling, leaving me stranded on the highway's center median. Cars sped by, occasionally slowing as the drivers peered at me and then hurried on. I could see the faces of the people passing in the oncoming lanes, and I knew they could see me as their expressions seemed to exclaim, "Glad, I'm not you!"

The crazy part is what happened next.

Nothing.

No one stopped to help. No Good Samaritan. No cop. No tow truck. The rain now came through the broken windows, shattered glass covered the seats, my shoulders were bruised, and my adrenaline pumped like water from a busted pipe. Still, no one stopped to help—not even the truck driver who almost certainly saw me career off the road.

I rummaged around and found my cell phone—dead battery. Of course.

After moments of feeling completely alone and helpless, I rummaged through the car to find a spiral-bound notebook and a Sharpie marker. I wrote in big letters "CALL HELP!" and held it up against the shattered windshield so oncoming traffic might stop gawking and do something useful.

Finally, more than half an hour later, a fire truck pulled up, and the firemen pried open the back doors of the car to see if I was OK. They called a tow truck, which arrived even later. I hitched a ride as my Suburban was towed to a repair shop, and then I waited another hour for my dad to retrieve me and take me home.

It was a long and harrowing ordeal, but I was grateful to be alive. Still, I will never forget those long minutes ticking by as I sat on the side of the road in the darkness of the stormy sky, feeling so alone. I desperately waited for someone—*anyone*—to come to my rescue.

GOD IS *ALWAYS* UP TO SOMETHING

The hardest part of suffering is how long it can last. Our battles seem to go on forever, and the soundtracks of anxiety, worry, depression, and fear only make these seasons feel more dramatic. The middle of angst is where the new you is made. God works in your waiting. You can despise this journey and the divine movement behind waiting…or you can lean in and realize that as you wait, God is working out something in you that cannot be formed any other way.

Last summer, my children had a moment of confusion as I baked them some chicken nuggets. Their dad suddenly went from standing by the oven to curled up in a ball in front of it. I was listening to a song from Shane and Shane in my headphones. It's the song "Though You Slay Me" with John Piper's voice dubbed over the bridge section.

If you haven't heard this amazing song, you need to look it up. Seriously, stop reading for a few minutes, grab your phone—you know it's already within arm's distance. Find this song and listen to it. I'll be here when you're done…

What'd you think? Great song, right? As the words hit my mind that day, my heart was crushed on the goodness of God. As Piper started speaking, I gasped for air and fell to the floor. It wasn't a moment of grief—it was a moment of *relief*. I realized that even if God was allowing my pain and suffering, He was all I needed in the midst of it.

Some of the most meaningful lyrics of the song for me are:

> *Though you slay me*
> *Yet I will praise you*
> *Though you take from me*
> *I will bless your name*
> *Though you ruin me*
> *Still I will worship*
> *Sing a song to the One who's all I need*

Through my sobs, I looked up at my five kids staring at me from the kitchen table with stunned looks on their faces.

"Daddy, did the chicken nuggets make you cry?"

"Dad, are you OK?"

"I am more than OK, kids. God's got me, even when I don't feel it."

THERE WILL BE A SLIGHT DELAY

In the moments when it feels like God is nowhere to be found, we grow frustrated and discouraged. No one wants to have to beg for something, especially from God. But we can trust that He is working and developing something in us even when we can't see it.

John Piper's powerful words in that song are from a sermon he preached in 2013.[1] Here they are again from the song:

Not only is all your affliction momentary, not only is all your affliction light in comparison to eternity and the glory there. But all of it is totally meaningful. Every millisecond of your pain, from the fallen nature or fallen man, every millisecond of your misery in the path of obedience is producing a peculiar glory you will get because of that.

Just because God is silent doesn't mean He is absent. He uses His silence as a way to bring us further into His presence. Frequently, He asks us to wait. We hate waiting when we don't understand the purpose behind it. If we know what we're waiting for, it suddenly makes sense to stay still.

Suppose you're at a restaurant and are ready to order. You're *so* hungry and can't wait to get that delicious hamburger you're craving. However, your server is nowhere around. You were seated at your table, given water and a menu, but no one ever came to take your order. The longer you wait, the more irritated you become. Now you're *hangry*.

Now imagine that you knew he was not helping you because of a valid reason. Perhaps he was helping a disabled, elderly lady to her car. What if he was getting you a new appetizer to try, on the house? What if he was giving the line chef a hand after he just spilled a five-gallon bucket of salsa on the kitchen floor?

Waiting is never enjoyable, but when you know the reason for it, you're much more patient and willing to sit tight. People wait in line for Black Friday deals, the latest Apple store gadget, a doctor they trust, or the release of a blockbuster movie. We don't mind waiting if we can anticipate the result.

I know what you're thinking: "But Josh, God doesn't always give us a reason…" You're right. He may not reveal why He has you waiting, but you know enough about Him that He always makes the wait worth it.

God's very character is that of a trustworthy, faithful, loving, and just Father (Exodus 34:6–7; Matthew 7:9–10; 1 John. 1:9). We wait on Him because we know His character to be true, His promises to be fulfilled, and His strength to be more than adequate.

As the people of Israel were in the midst of turmoil and waiting for God to save them, the prophet Isaiah said:

> Why do You say, O Jacob,
> and speak, O Israel,
> "My way is hidden from the Lord,
> and my right is disregarded by my God"?
> Have you not known? Have you not heard?
> The Lord is the everlasting God,
> the Creator of the ends of the earth.
> He does not faint or grow weary;
> His understanding is unsearchable (Isaiah 40:27–28).

We say the same thing as Jacob (a.k.a. Israel): "God doesn't care about me—my ways are hidden from Him." We think He has bigger problems to take care of in the universe, or we assume He just created us and walked away, leaving us to our messes. But Isaiah says, "God does care! Nothing is hidden from Him."

God never forgets His promises, never grows weary of handling details, and never shrugs off His children's needs. He never lacks the strength or desire to be involved in our lives. *Never.*

The human mind can't fathom how God keeps track of all the details in the lives of all His children. With the myriad problems and disasters around the world, how does He stay involved with it all? More specifically, how is He able to stay concerned about MY issues when the needs around the globe are so vast? Here's how:

"His understanding is unimaginable." We could try to comprehend it, but that's a futile task. There is no way to understand God's greatness and omnipotence fully, so we trust it.

WAITERS WANTED

God's character demands that I wait on Him. By waiting on God, I will have a fearless and faithful life—strength in suffering, peace in chaos.

Waiting on God means we can fully rest and rely on Him without any crutch for our faith. After explaining that God has strength enough for all of us, Isaiah goes on to say:

> They who wait for the Lord shall renew their strength; they shall mount up with wings like eagles; they shall run and not be weary; they shall walk and not faint (Isaiah 41:3).

"Wait" in this passage carries a beautiful meaning in the original Hebrew. It is not the idea of waiting with tapping fingers for God to come through. It is not the idea of standing in a queue in hopes that your number is called next. It doesn't make sense that waiting would renew strength if it were that kind of waiting.

This original idea of waiting here is to be "bound with" or "interwoven" like strands of a cord. When we wait on God, we are bound with Him. It provides us the strength this passage promises. Waiting on the Lord is actively growing in faith toward Him, not passively hoping He calls us next.

The way we muster strength is to wait on Him or, as another translation of Scripture simply puts it, "Trust in the Lord." It is an act of obedience with a great reward. The challenge and opportunity are to wait on God, not run ahead of Him or look beyond Him.

It means we wait without worrying. We grow anxious about nothing but trust God in everything.

Whether it's how the bills will be paid this week, how you'll find a job after looking for months, or how a broken relationship can be mended—in all things, we trust our all-powerful God to be our strength. Waiting on God is exercising confidence in His perfect timing.

Waiting on God shapes the new you.

You bind together with God, through Christ and the power of the Holy Spirit, to become an unstoppable force against any emotion and any circumstance.

Even anxiety.

HURRY UP AND WAIT

We live in a "microwave society"—we need *everything* in two minutes or less. When you're standing in a long line at the grocery store, someone is likely to start ranting about the lousy customer service and the lack of good help these days. If the car at the front of the intersection doesn't start moving a second after the light turns green, horns begin honking. Waiting can accelerate anxiety.

So when we hear that we're supposed to wait on God, it can rub us the wrong way. The ability to wait on the Lord stems from being confident and focused on who God is and in what He is doing. It means we're confident in His very nature. It means knowing and trusting in God's promises, purposes, and power.

In Isaiah's poetic language, he says we will "mount up with wings like eagles." Just as an eagle's feathers are made new through resting and waiting, we are given new wings to soar with perseverance through the battering winds of life. The fresh feathers of the eagle give a picture of being renewed with strength as the direct result of waiting on God.

The prophet goes on to write in the voice of God:

Fear not, for I am with you; be not dismayed, for I am your God; I will strengthen you, I will help you, I will uphold you with My righteous right hand (Isaiah 41:10).

The power and strength of Almighty God is your fuel for life. His strength demands your trust. Sometimes the Lord calms the storm. Sometimes He lets the storm rage and calms His child. All the while, He merely asks that you trust Him, waiting on Him to be your strength. Envision the new you—God is working all things together, and that vision is coming.

The end of your anxiety is to give you more of Christ. That is worth it all. Wait for it.

For still the vision awaits its appointed time;
it hastens to the end—it will not lie.
If it seems slow, wait for it;
it will surely come; it will not delay (Habakkuk 2:3).

THREE STEPS TOWARD THE END OF ANXIETY

PRAY

Ask for God to break any disillusionment that may be blocking you from seeing God's faithfulness in your life. Affirm to Him that you are willing to wait on His best plan for your life.

REFLECT

Remember what you are waiting for: God's way to win in your life. What promises from God are most helpful to you in your waiting? How have you seen the Lord's presence and activity as you wait?

ACT

Next time you are feeling anxious, worried, or fearful, commit to acting and thinking biblically before fear takes over. Think about the last time you experienced worry, fear, or panic. Where was your focus? What could you have done prior to the spike in anxiety that would have allowed you to handle those circumstances better? Commit to actions such as going for a prayer walk, writing in a prayer journal, or listening to a worshipful song.

LET IT BEGIN

You are not the first or the last person to deal with anxiety.

The good news is that you are not crazy, and you are not alone.

The bad news is that others are going to go through the same craziness you and I experience.

But we know the answer. We know how to help—or more importantly, we know *Who* can help. Anxiety can be used by God to make us more like Christ.

As we live out our faith in our struggles in this world, we can set an example for those who come after us. We can show them what it means to stay in perfect peace and be lifted up when our world is down.

Our healing found in Christ can point them to the One who can do more than they ever imagine.

WELCOME TO GRACE HOSPITAL

When arriving at a hospital, there is a clear distinction between who provides care and who needs care. The wounded are usually lying down, wearing odd hospital gowns, and tethered to some pole for monitoring their vital signs or IV fluids.

Pretend for a second that you are a patient in the hospital named *Grace*. Another patient, carried in by paramedics, soon fills the open bed next to you. On the count of three, they gently lift and place that person in the hospital bed beside you. After the caretakers leave with the proper wires and tubes in place, that person glances around at other patients and wonders if their conditions are worse or better.

Imagine that you briefly make eye contact with the new patient, share a short smile, and wait for each other to make small talk. No matter your condition or theirs, the reality is that you're both broken. Hurting in your own way, you're fighting for a healthier future. I'm in a bed fighting too, just a few rows over.

Grace Hospital is where the broken, hurting, disillusioned, weak, and spiritually emancipated ache for healing. In this hospital, we're all keenly aware of the help we need, even if we're not sure how to describe or understand the pain we're in right now.

Here we are, next to each other, not knowing exactly the level of pain or fear we may each be experiencing. As patients, we know that we do not have the answers to make each other well.

I'm not able to fix you.

You're not able to fix me.

What we do know with certainty is that Grace Hospital has the best Physician the world will ever know because He has helped many who have gone before us (see Hebrews 11 for a list of previous patients). As C.S. Lewis aptly put it in a letter to his once-hurting friend, "Think of me as a fellow patient in the same hospital who, having been admitted a little earlier, may be able to give some advice."[1] Our advice flows only from what we've already learned or experienced from the faithful hand of our Savior, the Great Physician.

At Grace, we are right where we belong. Here, no one is condemned for their cloud of depression, their fog of confusion, or their storm of anxiety. It is only inside Grace where we can experience the healing power needed to bring peace to our pains and hope for our losses.

It would be unloving to keep the help we find in the grace of Christ a secret. Instead, we must point others to the source of hope and peace that can only be found in God and God alone.

The greatest sign of health is when those who were once wounded turn around and help others. The best nurses were patients first. The best counselors needed counseling first. The best teachers were students first. The best followers of Jesus are those who remember who they were before Christ and with passion and urgency do everything they can to get others to the foot of the cross with them.

OUR CHIEF PURPOSE

What if the point of everything you've gone through or are going through is to help someone else find hope in Christ? What if this suffering is not just to make you more like Christ but to help others see Him as well?

Daniel and Rosie Henderson have become some of my dearest friends. Daniel is an author and served as a pastor for over twenty-five years. One night during a trial in our lives, Molly and I went over to their back porch and sat with them as they rocked back and forth in their classic white rocking chairs. I will never forget how Daniel recounted a season of anxiety and pain he had in his life as a way to let us know we were not alone and that we would survive this season.

At one point, he said to me, "If I went through all I did twenty years ago just to sit here and help you, it was all worth it." Only someone who has experienced brokenness can impart such beautiful grace. Only a man who understands that God can use pain for a greater purpose would say such a selfless statement.

Our chief purpose is to live out the Great Commandment and fulfill the Great Commission, regardless of our setbacks.

OUR CHIEF JOY

What if the point of everything you'll ever experience is to show you that your worst pain is not your anxiety but your lack of ability to trust Christ?

What if all of this was meant to create in you a desire to love God more?

The worst miseries in this life are not the anxieties we face; it is that we love Christ so little, though we are so greatly loved. C.H. Spurgeon shared this illustration with his students:

> A soul under special manifestations of love weeps that it can love Christ no more. Mr. Welch, a Suffolk minister, weeping at table, and being asked the reason of it, answered it was because he could love Christ no more. The true lovers of Christ can never rise high enough in their love to Christ. They count a little love to be no love, great love to be but little, strong love to be but weak, and the highest love to be infinitely below the worth of Christ, the beauty and glory of Christ, the fullness, sweetness, and goodness of Christ. The top of their misery in this life is that they love so little though they are so much beloved.[2]

OUR CHIEF END

What if the point of everything you'll ever experience is to arrive at glory and realize that what you endured was worth the suffering in exchange for Christ? Paul said it well in Romans 8:18: "For I consider that the sufferings of this present time are not worth comparing with the glory that is to be revealed to us." As we apply the principles we've explored on this journey together, we must remember above all to cling to Christ as we endure our present circumstances.

Jesus commanded:

> Therefore I tell you, do not be anxious about your life, what you will eat or what you will drink, nor about your body, what you will put on. Is not life more than food, and the body more than clothing? Look at the birds of the air: they neither sow nor reap nor gather into barns, and yet your heavenly Father feeds them. Are you not of more value than they? And which of you by being anxious can add a single hour to his span of life? (Matthew 6:25–27)

Jesus didn't mince words—believers are not to be controlled by anxiety.

But He didn't just say, *"Stop it."* He finished His words on anxiety by saying, "Seek first His Kingdom and His righteousness, and all these things will be added to you" (Matthew 6:33).

SEEK CHRIST FIRST

When we seek Christ first, all other demands and priorities fall into line behind the cross of Christ and His resurrection for our salvation.

Christ redirects our focus. He takes our eyes off our worries and onto His sufficiency. He promised that when we seek Him first, *all things* will be added to us. What things? A fuller and complete life, "peace peace," strength in waiting, purpose in pain, courage, and faith. When we seek His Kingdom first, all good, earthly things are an outflow of His grace over any fear, doubt, and anxiety we may ever encounter.

Press on, my friend. Your anxiety, worry, fear, stress, panic, and depression are not the end of you. In fact, it may be just the start of something great.

Remember, the chief end of anxiety is to glorify God and enjoy Him forever.

Your anxiety is not the end. It is only the beginning of His glory through you.

Press on with your eyes fixed on Christ: the end of your anxiety.

THANK YOUS . . .

T hank you, Jon Cook, for being a God-appointed writing partner. Thank you for your endless patience and for helping me capture the glory of Christ in the midst of my own wretchedness for the sake of helping others.

Thank you, Donna Cook, for cleaning up my grammatical wake and never complaining, just always making me better, for God's glory.

Thank you, Cassie Baker, for protecting my time, partnering with me in the daily mess of pastoral ministry, and encouraging me to never stop writing.

Thank you, Del and Diane, for providing your cottage as a place for my soul to meet with the Lord and write.

Thank you, Tim Peterson, for not giving up on me, having endless grace, and giving me another chance as a writer.

Thank you, Karla Dial, for intentionally surveying every word of this book to make it better.

Thank you, Alex Field, for believing in me when others didn't.

Thank you, Grace Chapel, for letting me live out my faith amidst such a loving body of believers.

Thank you, elders of Grace Chapel, for being my angels and believing my ministry isn't done yet.

Thank you, Randy Patten, for being the greatest mentor, friend, supervisor, and brother in Christ I could ever ask for.

Thank you, Mom and Dad. You have been faithful through every valley and mountain top. I love you.

Thank you, Chandler, Gracie, Carolina, Daisy, and Charlie. You show me Christ more than you know. I love you all, to the moon and back.

. . . For the glory of Christ Jesus, my Lord.

Lamentations 3:21-26

NOTES

CHAPTER 2

1. David Powlison and Paul David Tripp, "How to Care for Someone Battling Anxiety and Depression," Gospel Coalition, May 1, 2018, https://www.thegospelcoalition.org/podcasts/tgc-podcast/tripp-powlison-care-someone-battling-anxiety-depression.

CHAPTER 3

1. James Buckingham, "Wrestling with God," *Charisma Magazine*, 1991.
2. Ibid.
3. Charles Spurgeon, *The Complete Works of C.H. Spurgeon, Volume 41: Sermons 2394 to 2445* (Fort Collins, Colorado: Delmarva Publications, Inc., 2011).

CHAPTER 4

1. Max Lucado, *In the Grip of Grace: Your Father Always Caught You. He Still Does.* (Nashville, Tennessee: Thomas Nelson, 2011), 108.

CHAPTER 7

1. Lydia Brownback, *Finding God in My Loneliness* (Wheaton, Illinois: Crossway, 2017).
2. Elisabeth Elliot, *The Path of Loneliness: Finding Your Way through the Wilderness to God* (Ada, Michigan: Baker Publishing Group, 2007).

CHAPTER 8

1. Douglas Mangum, "Truth," *Lexham Theological Wordbook*, ed. Douglas Mangum et al. (Bellingham, Washington: Lexham Press, 2014).
2. William Arndt, Frederick W. Danker, and Walter Bauer, *A Greek-English Lexicon of the New Testament and Other Early Christian Literature* (Chicago: University of Chicago Press, 2000), 919.
3. Peter O'Brien, *The New International Greek Testament Commentary: The Epistle to the Philippians* (Grand Rapids, Michigan: William B. Eerdmans Publishing Company, 1991), 504.
4. G. Walter Hansen, *The Letter to the Philippians* (Grand Rapids, Michigan: William B. Eerdmans Publishing Company, 2009), 303.
5. Kevin M. Gilmartin, *Emotional Survival for Law Enforcement: A Guide for Officers and Their Families* (Tucson, Arizona: E-S Press, 2002), Chapter 5.

CHAPTER 9

1. Archibald Hart, *Overcoming Anxiety* (New York, New York: W Publishing Group, 1989), 9.
2. J. I. Packer, *Knowing God* (Westmont, Illinois: InterVarsity Press, 1993), 23.
3. John Murray, *Principles of Conduct: Aspects of Biblical Ethics* (Grand Rapids, Michigan: William B. Eerdmans Publishing Company, 1957), 236–37.

4. Paul David Tripp, *Awe: Why It Matters for Everything We Think, Say, and Do* (Wheaton, Illinois: Crossway, 2015).

CHAPTER 10

1. Stuart Scott, *Anger, Anxiety and Fear: A Biblical Perspective* (Bemidji, Minnesota: Focus Publishing, 2009).

CHAPTER 11

1. I heard the British preacher Graham Cooke preach a message on God's love once, and he said these lines, including "Because he loves you …" over and over and over. I began to weep. Sometimes we just need to hear this again, and again, and again…

CHAPTER 12

1. Based on information found in an article by Liora Nordenberg, "Dealing with the Depths of Depression," at the U.S. Federal Drug Administration website. Final Lincoln quote found at sermons.com.
2. C.S. Lewis, *A Grief Observed* (London: CrossReach Publications, 2016).

CHAPTER 13

1. Frederick William Danker, *The Concise Greek–English Lexicon of the New Testament* (Chicago: University of Chicago Press, 2009); BibleWorks, v.9.
2. Walter Bauer, *A Greek-English Lexicon of the New Testament and Other Early Christian Literature*, ed. Frederick W. Danker, 3rd ed. (Chicago: University of Chicago Press, 2000); BibleWorks, v. 9.
3. Timothy S. Lane and Paul David Tripp, *Relationships: A Mess Worth Making* (Greensboro, North Carolina: New Growth Press, 2006), 95.
4. Timothy Keller, *Walking with God through Pain and Suffering* (New York, New York: Viking Books, 2013).

CHAPTER 14

1. It is controversial whether Spurgeon ever said this. The closest citation I could find was in his 1874 sermon "Sin and Grace": "The wave of temptation may even wash you higher up upon the Rock of ages, so that you cling to it with a firmer grip than you have ever done before, and so again where sin abounds, grace will much more abound." Though it may not be directly tied to a quote on trials, the heart of what my brother was sharing with me is still the same.
2. H. D. M. Spence-Jones, ed., *Isaiah*, vol. 1 (London and New York, New York: Funk & Wagnalls Company, 1910), 414.

CHAPTER 16

1. John Piper, "The Glory of God in the Sign of Eternity," YouTube, October 2, 2013, https://www.youtube.com/watch?v=h8iEtbyzDLE. I assign this sermon as something for my biblical counseling cases to listen to; no matter what suffering you face, these words are powerful. I commend it to you!

EPILOGUE

1. Letter to Sheldon Vanauken from April 22, 1953, quoted in C.S. Lewis, *A Severe Mercy* (New York, New York: HarperOne, 2009), 134.
2. Charles Spurgeon, *Lectures to My Students: Volume 2* (Albany, Oregon: AGES Software, 1996), https://www.mat.univie.ac.at/~neum/sciandf/spurgeon/spurgeon2.pdf.